SO-EKL-316

PEACEFUL, POSITIVE REVOLUTION

Advanced Reading Copy

*Reviewers are reminded, this is an
uncorrected, digitally printed
limited edition and not for resale.*

*Final publication will include blurbs,
reviews and index.*

*If you would like consideration to be
included in the reviews of this book
please send your comments to:*

Tendril Press

PO Box 441110
Aurora, Colorado 80044
www.TendrilPress.com

PEACEFUL, POSITIVE REVOLUTION

ECONOMIC SECURITY FOR EVERY AMERICAN

STEVEN SHAFARMAN

DENVER, COLORADO

Peaceful, Positive Revolution:
Economic Security for Every American

Copyright © 2008 by Steven Shafarman. All Rights Reserved.

www.CitizenPolicies.org

Published by Tendril Press™
www.TendrilPress.com
PO Box 441110
Aurora, CO 80044
303.696.9227

No part of this publication may be reproduced, stored in a retrieval system, or transmitted in any form or by any means, electronic, mechanical, photocopying, or otherwise, without the prior written permission of Tendril Press, LLC and Steven Shafarman. The material in this book is furnished for informational use only and is subject to change without notice. Tendril Press assumes no responsibility for any errors or inaccuracies that may appear in the documents contained in this book.

All images, logos, quotes and trademarks included in this book are subject to use according to trademark and copyright laws of the United States of America.

ISBN 978-0-9802190-1-2 Paper

Printed in the United States of America
10 9 8 7 6 5 4 3 2 1

Art Direction, Book Design and Cover Design © 2008. All Rights Reserved by
A J Images Inc. Business Design & Publishing Center
www.AJImagesInc.com — 303•696•9227
info@AJImagesInc.com

For True Patriots

Contents

Part One
Our Lives

*W*e hold these truths to be self-evident, that all men are created equal, that they are endowed by their Creator with certain unalienable Rights, that among these are Life, Liberty and the pursuit of Happiness. That to secure these rights, Governments are instituted among Men, deriving their just powers from the consent of the governed. That whenever any Form of Government becomes destructive of these ends, it is the Right of the People to alter or to abolish it.

Declaration of Independence

1

Our Lives

Who knows what's best for you and your family? You and your family, of course.

What's best for your neighborhood, your community? It makes sense – doesn't it? – that you and your neighbors should decide.

Who decides for your town or city? Your state? Our nation? The United States of America was founded on the principle that sovereignty is in We the People — you and your family, your friends and neighbors and their neighbors, every U.S. citizen, all of us together. We the People decide.

That's the theory. As individuals, each of us is free, equal, endowed by our creator with unalienable rights, and encouraged to do what's best for ourselves and our families. Together, We the People are sovereign. We create our government. We make laws directly or through elected representatives. We select, instruct, and manage our representatives through politics.

In reality, however, very few of us participate actively in politics. Many of us don't even vote. We individuals are not doing our jobs as members of We the People.

According to the theory, our representatives do just that: they represent us. Their job is to carry our voice to the government, to help us do what's best for ourselves and our families, our neighborhoods and communities, our towns and cities and states and nation.

In reality, our elected representatives are professional politicians. Though most of them are good people with good intentions, they're preoccupied with campaigning for reelection or higher office. They're busy raising money, trying to get favorable publicity, working with party leaders and strategists, meeting with lobbyists for the special interests that fund their campaigns. They don't have much time for listening to us, their constituents.

Has an elected official ever asked you what you think, what you want? Did he or she listen to your response? Really listen, not just politely pretend to listen in order to get your vote or a campaign contribution? Did he or she vote or do as you requested?

There are plenty of reasons – good, sensible reasons – for not participating in politics. We're busy. We're pursuing happiness. We're working to earn enough money, caring for our families, relaxing with our friends, taking care of other business that's more urgent or more satisfying than politics. It takes time and effort to be an active, responsible citizen. The issues are complicated. The consequences of laws and regulations are hard to evaluate. News sources and media are biased. The volume of information is overwhelming. Politicians confound or mislead us, sometimes on purpose, sometimes without even trying.

Of course we want change. A lot of us are active in politics despite the challenges and frustrations. In addition, many of us perform community service, volunteering as tutors, in homeless shelters, for neighborhood cleanups, and countless other projects, with church groups and nonprofit agencies and on our own. Too often, though, we're too busy to volunteer. A common attitude is "let government handle it."

But government is not handling things. Or it's handling things badly. It primarily serves not our interests but the special interests. Special interests use it as a tool and a profit center. Our government – government of the people, by the people, for the people – is broken.

Tens of millions of us are trapped by poverty and debt. Health care is frighteningly expensive. Millions of our children are badly educated. Taxes are high, and government wastes a lot of our money. Our air and water are polluted and our planet is heating up. Forests and wetlands are being destroyed. Species are going extinct. Our cities are decaying and sprawling, the roads choked with traffic. Injustice persists regarding race, gender, class, ethnic background, and sexual orientation. Terrorists may be lurking everywhere, and despite massive investments in national security we're still sitting ducks.

Is this what We the People want? Do we consent to being governed so badly? Are we content?

What about you, personally? Are you content? Do you consent? Is the current political system working for you and your family?

2

Citizen Policies

How can We the People be more successful in our sovereign role of governing ourselves? How can We the People and we individuals get the government we want?

Thomas Jefferson, Abraham Lincoln, Franklin Roosevelt, and Martin Luther King Jr. had an idea about that. So did many other people, including Richard Nixon, and he presented a detailed plan: a majority of Americans supported it; major newspaper editorials endorsed it; and the U.S. House of Representatives passed it, by a margin of two to one, but it was narrowly defeated in the Senate. We can update their idea.

It's a commonsense idea: guarantee people's economic security. A simple way to do that is with "Citizen Dividends" — a modest guaranteed income for every adult citizen.

Citizen Dividends should be enough for food and shelter, but just enough, a safety net, between $500 and $1,000 a month. There will still be strong incentives to work and earn more. By including all adult citizens and giving each of us the same basic income, we can create a baseline of economic justice and economic equality, while also promoting national unity and national security.

This is not socialism. Citizen Dividends will preserve private property and free enterprise. And enhance individual freedom and dignity. And increase personal responsibility. And create economic opportunities. And stimulate markets. And strengthen our democracy.

Citizen Dividends, in fact, will produce a more ideal form of capitalism, more inclusive and therefore more fair and more just. Every citizen will have some capital. Every citizen will be able to participate freely in the market. Every citizen will have a greater sense of ownership, of being a stakeholder or shareholder in America.

Does $1,000 a month for you and every other adult American sound like pie in the sky, too good to be true?

We can afford Citizen Dividends without raising taxes. The money will come from cutting government programs that become superfluous, starting with individual welfare and corporate welfare and the associated bureaucracies.

One of the fundamental purposes of government, according to our Constitution, is to "promote the general welfare." Citizen Dividends will do that directly, efficiently. And only that. Most government programs do not promote the *general* welfare; instead, they promote the *special* welfare of specific groups, businesses, industries, or communities. Dozens of current programs will become unnecessary; we'll be able to eliminate them. Many programs feature tax credits and deductions, so eliminating programs will facilitate tax reform, including tax cuts.

Citizen Dividends will immediately and significantly reduce poverty. That means there will be real progress on homelessness, hunger, health care, crime, and other issues or problems related to poverty. We'll also be able to relieve or prevent the economic disruptions that result from inflation, business cycles, and rising gasoline prices. Individuals and families will be better able to plan and budget.

It will be easier to live in accordance with moral and spiritual values when economic security is guaranteed in good times and bad. There won't be so much worrying about money. We'll be more free to devote our time and attention to family, friends, community, religious faith, creative pursuits, making a better world for ourselves and our posterity. Families will be stronger, as well, because husbands and wives will be able to afford more time to be together and with their children.

People will be able to invest personal time and effort, also, to attend town meetings, write to elected officials, volunteer in their communities, help strengthen the social fabric of our nation. Citizen Dividends will buy back a bit of everyone's time for the common good.

Some Americans already get extra income from the government. Every year, residents of Alaska get a share of oil royalties paid to the state. It was $1,654 per person in 2007. The Alaska Permanent Fund was created by an amendment to the state's constitution in 1980. Annual dividends have been paid since 1982.

Political efforts to guarantee economic security started with Thomas Jefferson. In 1776, he called on the Virginia legislature to give homesteads to people without property. Thomas Paine proposed a national fund that would make a cash payment to everyone at the age of 21 and yearly starting at age 50 as "a right, and not a charity." Abraham Lincoln sponsored the National Homestead Act; Congress passed it, and it provided land through four decades to more than 700,000 families. Populists and Progressives in the 1890s campaigned for greater economic security and won many political reforms. In 1935, millions of Americans supported the Townsend Plan Movement, which sought a secure income for seniors; millions more joined Share Our Wealth, the income redistribution movement led by Huey Long; goaded by their demands, our government enacted Social Security. Franklin Roosevelt asserted that "true individual freedom cannot exist without economic security and independence."

Advocates for "guaranteed income" or a "negative income tax" in the 1960s included more than 1,200 economists, from John Kenneth Galbraith on the left to Milton Friedman on the right. Martin Luther King Jr. called guaranteed income a necessary step toward solving problems of housing, education, and racial injustice. Lyndon Johnson appointed a commission of prominent businessmen, scholars, and union officials to study the idea; their report was unanimous, and recommended "the adoption of a new program of income supplementation for all Americans in need," *without any work requirement.*

Richard Nixon tried to reform welfare with his Family Assistance Plan to provide guaranteed cash payments to poor families. The House of Representatives passed it by a vote of 288-132. In the Senate, however, the plan and its moderate supporters – Democrats and Republicans – were narrowly defeated by the combined votes of extreme conservatives, who opposed any aid to the poor, and extreme liberals, who wanted the payments to be much larger.

In the next presidential election, 1972, George McGovern sought a more generous guarantee, "Demogrants," but his plan was mostly ignored. That was during the Vietnam war. There was turmoil in the McGovern campaign, the Democratic party, and our nation as a whole. Nixon was reelected. He did not reintroduce the Family Assistance Plan.

Our government provided guaranteed income to thousands of poor families between 1968 and 1975. In a series of "income maintenance experiments" in communities around the country, the federal Office of Economic Opportunity gave people enough money each month to ensure that they did not fall below some percent of the poverty level. Researchers tracked the recipients, monitoring the number of hours people worked, the rate of divorce, and other variables. During the debates about Nixon's plan, even though the experiments were far from concluded, some senators demanded the results. The preliminary data indicated an increase in divorce and decline in total work hours. Opponents of the plan touted those "facts," and used them to defeat it.

In the final analysis, the rate of divorce was no different than comparison groups. Total work hours declined about 6 percent. The experiments did not document reasons for the decline. There was evidence that husbands left bad jobs to look for better ones; wives devoted more time to their families; teenagers stayed in school, and got better grades.

Nixon's Family Assistance Plan – which was created by Daniel Patrick Moynihan, who wrote a book about it, *The Politics of a Guaranteed Income* – was terribly complicated. It was only for the very poor, with strict means-testing. It would have excluded single adults, varied the payments according to recipients' income and family size, and penalized unemployed recipients who did not participate in job-training programs.

Citizen Dividends will be perfectly simple. Every adult citizen will receive the same basic income.

Think about how this could help poor families meet critical needs. Think about how it could help middle class families realize their dreams.

Think about it, also, personally: What could you do with an extra $500 to $1,000 a month?

Suppose you get that every month, tax-free. Suppose your spouse gets the same amount. So do each of your parents and your adult children.

How might that benefit you and your family? What would it mean for the quality of your life today? How would it affect your dreams, hopes, and plans for the future?

Citizen Service

In return for Citizen Dividends, would you be willing to perform some "Citizen Service" in your community?

You could serve in many different ways, say eight hours each month, according to your interests and schedule. You might volunteer in your child's or grandchild's classroom or school PTA, train with the police or fire department to assist in emergencies, care for an elderly neighbor or disabled relative, plant trees and help maintain a neighborhood park or garden, work with a church group or nonprofit agency, serve on a jury, join a community board or commission.

Community service is a favorite theme of Bill Clinton, Colin Powell, and Ralph Nader, among many other 21st-century leaders. Service, they tell us, makes communities more livable, reduces demand for government programs, educates volunteers to be responsible citizens, inspires recipients to serve other people, reminds each of us that we are part of the larger community, inspires feelings of pride in the community and our nation. Citizen Service will provide these benefits for all of us.

Service and charity are important values in our Christian, Jewish, Muslim, and secular traditions. Giving of our time is a much more meaningful form of charity than just giving money.

Millions of Americans already do some volunteer work on a weekly, monthly, or annual basis. What about you?

Among people who do not volunteer, many more would choose to — if they could afford the time. Citizen Dividends will make universal community service possible.

It might seem that some government agency would be required to monitor and certify our monthly service. Would you need to be supervised like that? Would you shirk that duty? The vast majority of Americans are basically honest and responsible. Instead of a big, expensive bureaucracy, Citizen Service would rely on social pressure. Social pressure is extremely powerful. And it's free.

In the 1960s debates about guaranteed income, some opponents denounced it as "giving people something for nothing." With Citizen Service, people will be giving something back to their communities, something significant. Citizen Service will also substitute for some government programs, at least partially, thereby facilitating government budget cuts. Combining Citizen Service and Citizen Dividends is a practical way to get serious about "compassionate conservatism." It's also an affordable way to create an absolute social safety net, the ideal of liberalism.

Think about your neighborhood and what it could be when residents are performing eight hours or more of service each month. Envision local schools when mentors are available for every child who needs one, and every classroom teacher has the assistance of other adults. Imagine senior centers, public hospitals, and group homes for people with disabilities, each with plenty of volunteer caregivers. Picture well-maintained and improved parks, gardens, libraries, and other public assets. Think about our added security when volunteers are trained and available to work with police, firefighters, and other professionals whenever there's an emergency. Consider how increased citizen involvement can make local governments more open, accountable, effective, and democratic.

Are there service activities you might find meaningful? Secular or religious charities or civic associations you could join and work with? Community enhancements you want, but right now you just can't afford the time to work on?

Would you be more willing and able to volunteer if you were getting Citizen Dividends?

Citizen Policies

The combination of Citizen Dividends and Citizen Service will empower ordinary Americans – each of us, all of us – economically and politically. These "Citizen Policies" will remind every adult every month that we are stakeholders.

Of course we're not the only stakeholders. Children are stakeholders, too. And children will benefit in many ways from Citizen Policies. When parents can afford to spend more time with their families, children will be more safe and secure, physically, socially, and emotionally. More time with their parents means more opportunities for children to learn from their parents and absorb their parents' values. Children will no longer be ashamed or stigmatized if their families receive public assistance, because this universal social safety net eliminates the stigma – along with the coercion, inefficiency, and corruption – that currently comes with public assistance programs.

In addition, every child will know that basic economic security is guaranteed, and that he or she will start getting Citizen Dividends at age 18. That knowledge will give children the courage to pursue education, careers, and lives that fulfill their dreams. Their parents, too, and the rest of us regardless of our ages and family situations, will also find it easier to pursue our dreams.

Our lives will be better. Our world will benefit enormously. Our government will become more responsive, accountable, and democratic — more truly ours.

3

Frequently Asked Questions

How large should Citizen Dividends be?

Enough to meet basic costs of food and shelter, but just enough — a basic income. Between $500 and $1,000 a month. (If it's $860 a month for each adult, the total is $20,640 a year for a couple. The poverty level is $20,650 for a family of four, according to the U.S. Census Bureau.)

Whatever the amount, some people will want it to be more; others will consider it excessive. It will have to be adjusted periodically, when economic and political conditions change. There might be supplements, using local funds, in places where the cost of living is high.

Can we afford that? What about the national debt and federal budget deficits?

Yes we can afford it. Citizen Dividends will cost less than the current programs they replace.

Plus, it will become much easier for us to manage the debt and reduce deficits. Citizen Policies will facilitate cutting government programs. We'll be able to implement fiscal and political reforms that are currently blocked by special interests.

We *cannot* afford to persist with policies that are failing to promote the general welfare.

(More information about how we can pay for Citizen Dividends is in Appendix 2.)

Won't this undermine people's reasons and incentives to work? What if people quit their jobs?

Would you quit your job? Would you choose to live on less than $1,000 a month? Why, when you can have that added to your current income? Won't you still want to work and earn more?

Americans characteristically have a strong work ethic. Citizen Dividends that meet only basic needs will leave the work ethic intact. There will still be many good reasons and real incentives to work, earn, compete, and produce. Work will still be meaningful — it may even be more meaningful. People will continue to have goals, dreams, and desires that involve working and earning more money.

The only incentives that will be undermined are those that rely on fear — fear of hunger, fear of homelessness, fear of humiliation and other hardships. That's the coercion ethic. The coercion ethic is very different from the work ethic. Coercion can counteract the work ethic. When people are coerced, many of us become angry, defiant, or depressed, and less motivated to work and produce. Undermining the coercion ethic will liberate the work ethic and allow the work ethic to flourish.

What if some people quit their jobs anyway? Won't that be bad for our society?

It could be very good. Think about it:

The unemployment rate will go down, because other people will take the vacated jobs, and the official statistic only counts those who are actively looking for work. Inflation will also go down, because people who quit will have to be more thrifty. If people are being thrifty and consuming less gasoline, there will be less traffic, less urban sprawl, less pollution, slower global warming. Parents will spend more time with their children. Teens and young adults – and older people, too – will stay in school or go back to school. Some people will start new businesses, their own businesses, creating more new jobs for others.

Everyone who quits a job will still have some income for food and shelter. They won't be an added burden on the rest of us. It won't be necessary for our government to provide them with extra funds or services.

Are sufficient funds really available from cutting individual welfare and corporate welfare?

Yes. Several scholars have asked that question, done detailed analyses, and confirmed the financial feasibility:

- Irwin Garfinkel, at Columbia University, examined several models for eliminating existing welfare programs and distributing the money directly to everyone equally. Just doing that, he found, would cut the poverty rate in half.

- Michael L. Murray, formerly of Drake University College of Business and Public Administration, identified cuts sufficient to make monthly payments totaling $6,000 a year to every adult plus $2,000 a year for each child.

- Charles M. A. Clark, at St. John's University, has shown how we can provide a poverty level basic income and pay for it with a flat income tax of 35 percent.

- Allan Sheahen, with the U.S. Basic Income Guarantee Network, wants to give every citizen $10,000 a year, starting at age 18. He would pay for it by simplifying the tax code, reversing the Bush administration's tax cuts for the rich, and cutting wasteful government programs.

- Charles Murray, of the American Enterprise Institute, has a plan to give $10,000 a year to every citizen age 21 or over. He wants to end all other federal, state, and local programs that transfer funds, including Social Security, with a constitutional amendment to enforce the elimination of those programs. He would also eliminate Medicare and Medicaid; with the extra income people receive, everyone could afford medical insurance, and he would require everyone to buy it.

(References and more details are in Appendix 2.)

Each of these scholars examined only the federal budget, leaving out the savings from cutting state and local programs that also become superfluous. None of them calculated the significant savings from cutting corporate welfare, which is roughly $250 billion a year. None of their proposals included the concept of Citizen Service and the benefits and savings it will provide.

There's more than enough money available. The obstacles are entirely political. And politics is us.

Everyone talks about cutting government, and it never happens. How will Citizen Policies change that?

It hasn't happened because every government program serves some special interest or several special interests. Special interests, when defending their profits and privileges, are focused, organized, and disciplined. In contrast, the general interest and common causes of We the People are diffuse and disorganized. Individual people are easily distracted.

Do you want government to be more efficient, more cost-effective, more fiscally responsible? Almost all of us do. Politicians say they do, too.

With Citizen Policies, each of us will be getting monthly reminders that we are stakeholders. Each of us will have guaranteed economic security, independent of any job or other income as part of some special interest. Each of us will know that making government smaller and more efficient is in our personal interest, and could put more money in our pockets. Each of us will be actively serving our communities. Each of us, consequently, in many ways, will be more encouraged to recognize and identify with the general interest, the common good — We the People.

Real cuts will become possible because we – as individuals and together as We the People – will be more motivated to demand them and more able to organize ourselves to get them. Citizen Policies may be the only way to make real cuts and enact other reforms.

No new taxes?

We can do this with the current tax system, yes, with no new taxes.

We can also do it with a flat income tax. Or a national sales tax. Or a tax on consumption of natural resources. Or some other tax policy or combination of tax policies.

Tax reform will be much easier to enact if we start with Citizen Policies. That's because the current system is a gold mine for lots of special interests, which lobbied for the loopholes that make income taxes so complicated, intrusive, and abusive. Special interests usually manage to block reforms – including reforms that would close loopholes and enhance fairness – by denouncing them as "new taxes" or "tax increases."

Strict opposition to new taxes is good for the special interests that profit from the status quo. But it's bad for us ordinary citizens and bad for our government.

Isn't health care a necessity? Shouldn't Citizen Dividends be large enough so everyone can afford it? Or shouldn't we reform health care first, so everyone has it?

Concern about health care is a good reason to enact Citizen Policies right away.

Everyone will have extra income for health care or medical insurance. It will therefore be possible to debate reform proposals with less urgency and more prudence, and perhaps to test alternative reforms in different states. Concerned individuals will be in a better position to take the time to participate in the discussion. We the People will be more likely to prevail over the insurance and pharmaceutical industries.

Health care costs will be lower, because poverty and poor health are strongly correlated. There will be significant progress, as measured by premature births, premature deaths, and preventable diseases including HIV/AIDS.

Citizen Policies could be the key to successful health care reform.

What about the idea that government should provide jobs or create jobs, but should not provide income?

We hear that so often, it sounds so sensible, so right. Creating jobs, we're told, leads to more and faster economic growth, which leads to more tax revenues, which provide funds for national security, education, etc., which benefit everyone. Right? Isn't that what politicians and pundits tell us? Our government, in other words, creates jobs in order to carry out its constitutional mandate to promote the general welfare.

Government spending to create jobs is good for the people who get the jobs, of course, and good for the communities where the money is spent. That means it's very good for the elected officials who represent those people and communities. But what about the rest of us? Is it a wise use of our taxpayer dollars?

When we stop, think, ask questions, and do some research, here's what we find: "Creating jobs" means giving our tax money to private corporations that are supposed to hire people. We're paying the CEOs' salaries and the investors' stock dividends. We're rewarding special interests, increasing their profits, promoting their special welfare. In most cases, "creating jobs" is a euphemism for corporate welfare.

There's nothing in the Constitution about creating or providing jobs. The word "jobs" is not used, not even once. There's also nothing about "the economy" or "economic growth." Moreover and more important, government spending to create jobs usually fails to provide lasting benefits; it doesn't work.

We can promote the general welfare directly, more affordably and more effectively, with Citizen Dividends. Everyone will have real economic security. Those among us who are unemployed will have income for food and shelter while looking for jobs or creating their own jobs. There won't be any reason to expect government to create any extra jobs for anyone.

Our government will operate much more efficiently and productively. It will no longer be burdened by trying to create jobs.

Isn't it bad for people to be on the dole? Won't getting a check from the government every month lead to dependency and a sense of entitlement?

People say we Americans are naturally independent and should be independent, and that dependency is bad or wrong, a sign of weakness. But no one is truly independent. Regardless of what anyone says, the truth is that we need one another. We are mutually interdependent. It makes sense to acknowledge that openly and honestly.

Courts have ruled consistently that government must provide decent food and shelter to convicted felons in prison and to enemy prisoners of war. If people who have acted against the interests of society are so entitled, aren't you?

The United States of America was founded on the principle of universal entitlement: our "unalienable rights" to life, liberty, and the pursuit of happiness. Life requires food and shelter. Citizen Dividends will ensure that each of us has money for food and shelter. Each of us, and therefore all of us, will be more able to enjoy liberty. And more free to pursue happiness.

A sense of entitlement is only a real problem when some people claim or appear to be more entitled than others, to be entitled at the expense of others. That won't happen with Citizen Dividends. Citizen Dividends will be universal and equal.

What about people who are lazy or irresponsible? What about alcoholics and drug addicts? Why should we give them any money?

Would you forego Citizen Dividends – and the benefits to yourself, your family, and our society as a whole – just to stop a few people from wasting or misusing the money?

It's not as if current social and economic policies are preventing laziness, irresponsibility, and addiction. And it's not as if Citizen Dividends will promote such behavior. On the contrary, such behavior may decrease because guaranteed economic security will reduce or end the despair that commonly underlies it.

People who are lazy, irresponsible, or addicted won't have any claim on other government funds or services, and they won't be homeless, hungry, or begging on the streets. They won't be an added burden or nuisance for you and your family. You won't be bothered by them. You won't have to worry about them, unless you choose to become involved.

Many such people have reformed and transformed their lives, becoming productive citizens and contributing to society. We can give everyone the opportunity to better themselves. Such people might be helped through Citizen Service by their friends, families, neighbors, and communities.

Shouldn't parents with young children get a larger amount? What about single parents? What about orphans? What about children who have been abused, neglected, or abandoned?

We could give more money to parents with young children, of course, though that would complicate the program and compromise its essential egalitarianism. There are many other ways to assist parents and children. We could, for example, have fully refundable child tax credits. We could provide complete health care for children and pregnant women.

For single parents, some or all of the absent parent's Citizen Dividends could be redirected to pay child support. Courts might order that routinely. Single parents and their children – and their extended families, and our society as a whole – won't have to be so concerned about deadbeats.

For orphans and abused, neglected, or abandoned children: People will be more able and might be more eager to adopt, become foster parents, or find other ways to help, perhaps as their Citizen Service.

What about the very rich? Why should we give any money to Bill Gates?

How would you exclude him?

To screen out the small percentage of the population that really doesn't need any extra money would require means-testing, regulations, and a large expensive bureaucracy. The process would cost more money than it saves. In addition, excluding the very rich would trigger continual political disputes about where and how to draw the line. Including everyone will help end class warfare — for good.

Is the notion of giving a few hundred bucks a month to Bill Gates so distasteful? Is that a valid reason, in your opinion, to reject the significant benefits for all of us, including you?

What about immigrants?

U.S. citizenship is special. Citizen Policies will highlight that fact by drawing a sharp line between citizens and noncitizens.

For immigrants, Citizen Dividends will be an extra incentive to become citizens, if they can. Those who came here illegally, in most cases, are not eligible for citizenship.

After we enact Citizen Policies, everyone who's already a citizen will have extra income and greater economic security. There won't be so much fear of immigrants taking people's jobs. We'll be able to debate immigration and related issues more thoughtfully, responsibly, and productively.

What about people who are in prison? What about criminals who are paroled or on probation?

People in prison get food and shelter, so it makes sense to redirect their Citizen Dividends toward paying those costs. When prisoners are released, we can help them resume their lives and stay out of trouble by promptly restoring their Citizen Dividends to them.

For crimes that do not involve jail time, and for people who have been paroled or are on probation, courts could redirect some of the money to pay fines, penalties, and victim restitution. In many cases today it's impossible to collect fines or civil judgments because criminals are poor and have no income. Redirecting Citizen Dividends will serve justice, while reducing the social and monetary costs of crime.

There will also be a strong deterrent effect. People who might be tempted to commit crimes will have guaranteed income and economic security — but only if they continue to obey the law. And they'll know it.

What about the high cost of living – especially the cost of housing – in New York City, San Francisco, Washington, D.C., and other places? Would people who live there get more money?

Local or state governments could choose to supplement Citizen Dividends using local or state funds. If residents want that, they'll have to demand it. In cities, counties, or states with a high cost of living, voters might choose to provide supplements in order to keep residents from moving away.

Some elderly or handicapped people are unable to perform Citizen Service. Will they still get Citizen Dividends?

Yes. Of course. Citizen Dividends will be what Thomas Paine called for, "a right, and not a charity." Besides, hardly anyone is really incapable of performing some kind of service to the community. People who use wheelchairs, for example, or who have impaired vision or hearing, can still do tutoring, mentoring, and much more.

What if people don't perform Citizen Service? Some people are lazy or irresponsible. Some are rich or famous and might say they're too busy. Shouldn't it be mandatory?

Would you need it to be mandatory? Would you shirk if it's not?

What about your friends and neighbors? Do you think they'd shirk? If any of them did, would you talk to them about it?

Social pressure is powerful, often more effective than laws and regulations. There are lots of ways to invite, entice, inspire, and motivate people to participate as citizens. And that will be much easier when we have Citizen Dividends and everyone can afford the time to serve. There are also lots of ways to shame, embarrass, guilt-trip, and ostracize anyone who shirks.

Making Citizen Service mandatory would require laws, regulations, and verification procedures, with a big, expensive government bureaucracy. Besides, as we know from jury duty, people who are determined to shirk will do so despite the fact that service is mandatory and enforced by serious penalties.

People who are rich or famous, or want to be rich or famous, are especially responsive to social pressure. Movie and TV stars, professional athletes, politicians, CEOs, billionaires – anyone and everyone who's liable to get media attention and wants it to be favorable – will have to perform Citizen Service with the rest of us. It will be in their self-interest.

I see how this will be good for poor and middle-class Americans, and why they are likely to support it. What about the very rich? Won't they be opposed?

Even though the very rich are doing very well with the status quo, that's no reason to assume they oppose the general welfare. The very rich, after all, have a lot to lose if our social, cultural, and environmental problems worsen.

The very rich also have a lot to gain from increasing social and economic stability. Some are sure to recognize the benefits. They may be leading advocates.

If we eliminate corporate welfare subsidies and tax breaks, won't the stock market crash?

Some stock prices will fall. Other stocks will go up, particularly shares in corporations that were not getting government subsidies. More important, Citizen Policies will promote long-term stability – social, political, economic, and environmental – and consequently stock market growth that is more sustainable and better attuned to the real interests of most Americans.

What if there's an economic downturn or slowdown? Or a recession?

In any downturn or recession, Citizen Dividends will protect everyone from job losses and other hardships. Traditional efforts to end recessions rely on putting more money into circulation by cutting taxes, lowering interest rates, or increasing government spending. With each of these devices, the results are delayed, indirect, unreliable, and unevenly distributed. That's why it can take years for society to recover from a recession — and why some individuals and families never recover.

After we have Citizen Dividends, it will be possible to end recessions by increasing the amount of guaranteed income. That will put more money into circulation promptly, directly, reliably, and universally.

One of the few things almost all economists agree on: occasional downturns and recessions are unavoidable. That's a good reason to enact Citizen Policies quickly.

What about inflation? Won't adding Citizen Dividends to the economy cause prices to increase?

We won't just be adding Citizen Dividends; we'll be cutting existing subsidies and entitlements at the same time, offsetting the addition. That can be a smooth transition if government and the Federal Reserve Board act responsibly, if we are vigilant and demand that they act responsibly. The transition might be smoothed even more by introducing Citizen Dividends in phases, starting with the very poor or an amount that's less than desired.

If there is inflation after that – from any cause, at any time – we'll be able to adjust the amount of Citizen Dividends to prevent further problems.

How will Citizen Dividends be distributed?

Let's focus on the basic idea first.

Do you think this makes sense? Do you want a national conversation about Citizen Policies? That's the first step, conversation — ordinary citizens discussing this idea among ourselves, with our friends, co-workers, neighbors, and so on, including journalists and politicians.

If we decide to go ahead, working out the details will be easy. We can use automatic bank deposits, debit cards, income tax deductions and refunds. Because Citizen Dividends will be universal, with no means-testing, the process of distributing the money will be relatively simple, with very low administrative costs — unlike existing welfare programs. Conditional programs are complicated, with lots of loopholes and big bureaucracies, and therefore lots of waste and lots of potential for fraud.

It's important to focus on the idea of Citizen Dividends and not get caught up in questions of micromanagement. Special interests that profit from the status quo will try to distract us with discussions about the details, delaying progress while they continue to profit. That's a common political tactic and it usually succeeds. Advocates of Citizen Policies have to be prepared.

Could we do this in just one state? Can we try that first, and see how it works?

Yes. One state could do this.

Advocates might work to enact it in their state by, among other things, encouraging candidates for state and local offices to promise to make it their top priority. Advocates might become candidates, running for office on this platform. The state that does it first will get a great deal of attention from people in other states and countries.

It might even be possible to do it in a city or county — for example, a community where the federal government is closing a military base. The government tries to smooth the transition by giving subsidies to private companies that promise to create jobs. Instead, some of the money that was funding the base could be distributed directly for a few years to residents of the affected community.

Local Citizen Policies might also make sense after a major natural disaster. Recall Hurricane Katrina and the flooding of New Orleans. Our federal government appropriated $110 billion to start, and the cleanup and restoration will take many years and more billions. Federal officials managed these funds. A lot of the money went to big corporations with political connections. Many billions of dollars were wasted. Displaced residents had to cope with bureaucratic obstacles, errors, and delays; a lot of deserving people received little or no assistance.

In future disasters, residents of the affected area could get a few hundred dollars a month for some period. People will get money when they most need it — right away. They will decide how to rebuild their lives. Many of them will hire local companies, their neighbors, thereby speeding economic recovery. Local democracy will be strengthened. Even if some people misuse the money, there won't be large-scale abuses, like after Katrina, because no one will be getting that much.

Enacting Citizen Policies in a state – or a city, county, or region, perhaps after a natural disaster or military base closure – is workable. We could do that as a test, while we consider a national program.

Is there anything like this in any other country?
Not yet, though several countries are moving in this direction:

- Brazil enacted a law in 2004 declaring that everyone has a right to a minimum income. More than 11 million poor families were getting cash assistance in 2006, and that was a factor in the reelection of President Luis Inacio Lula da Silva that October.

- In South Africa in 2002, a government commission endorsed a plan to provide a monthly "basic income grant" to everyone age 7 or older. Supporters include Nobel Peace Prize winner Archbishop Desmond Tutu, along with many religious groups, labor unions, and social justice organizations. But President Thabo Mbeki opposed it.

- Prime Minister Pascoal Mocumbi of Mozambique endorsed the basic income grant in 2002. He declared it a necessary first step toward providing health care and education. Mozambique, however, is highly indebted, and government policies are constrained by the World Bank and International Monetary Fund.

- In Ireland, Germany, Australia, and other countries, elected officials have called for a basic income. Social programs are being cut in those countries, and people see basic income as a way to prevent or undo any damage.

There are many countries that provide or guarantee food, shelter, health care, and education. But in France, the Netherlands, and the Scandinavian countries, governments are relatively socialistic and paternalistic, with massive bureaucracies and very high taxes. Citizen Policies will minimize government and facilitate tax cuts.

In Kuwait, Qatar, Brunei, and other wealthy oil-producing countries, there are generous benefits for members of the ruling families and males of the dominant ethnic group, but only for them. Citizen Policies will include everyone.

The existing program most like Citizen Dividends is in Alaska. The Alaska Permanent Fund Dividend was established in 1980 to distribute oil royalties directly to the people. Annual dividends have been paid since 1982. In 2007, every legal resident of Alaska got $1,654. It's called the *Permanent* Fund because royalties are invested and only partly distributed, and dividends will continue even after the oil runs out. Social scientists have found that most Alaskans use the money responsibly to pay bills, invest in education, or save for retirement.

In every other state, the income gap between the very rich and everyone else has widened significantly since the 1970s. Alaska is the only state with reduced income inequality, a smaller income gap. That's because of these dividends.

This makes sense. Will the American people accept it?

Do you? Will your friends and neighbors? Who are "the American people" anyway?

Residents of Alaska accepted the Permanent Fund Dividend. There was a referendum on it in 1999 — and 83 percent voted to keep it unchanged. They love it.

Do you remember the $300 rebate checks that almost all taxpayers received in 2001? That was a key part of the first round of tax cuts Congress passed after George W. Bush took office. Did you accept the money? Do you know anyone who didn't? Is there some reason to think people would reject the idea of getting more than that every month?

What about the 2008 rebate checks? Many rejection or complaints?

Questions about what people want or will accept are usually answered through opinion polls or focus groups. Those procedures are paid for by clients with a vested interest, and can be designed to elicit particular responses. People and groups that profit from the status quo will spend many millions of dollars to confuse, distract, and mislead us. They'll conduct polls, hire lobbyists, hire economists, call for studies and hearings, insist that we can't afford it, denounce it as socialism. Every delay means more profits for them.

It's important to educate ourselves and others before we are distracted by polls and "experts." The best way to educate ourselves is to make these ideas personal. Think about your hopes and dreams. Imagine what it would mean for you and your family to have Citizen Policies. Talk to your family members, friends, and neighbors about these possibilities. Encourage them to dream and imagine, to make these ideas personal, and to help spread the word.

You and your family, your friends and neighbors and their neighbors — we are the American People. It will happen if We the People demand it.

Part Two
Our World

Guaranteed income would not only establish freedom as a reality rather than a slogan, it would also establish a principle deeply rooted in Western religious and humanist tradition: man has the right to live, regardless! This right to live, to have food, shelter, medical care, education, etc., is an intrinsic human right that cannot be restricted by any condition, not even the one that he must be socially 'useful.'

Erich Fromm

The danger that we would be underwriting the failures is trivial compared with the benefits the guaranteed annual income would provide us. It would provide dignity for every citizen and choice for every citizen.

Margaret Mead

The advantages of this arrangement [the negative income tax] are clear. It is directed specifically at the problem of poverty. It gives help in the form most useful to the individual, namely, cash. It is general and could be substituted for the host of special measures now in effect. It makes explicit the cost borne by society. It operates outside the market.

Milton Friedman

The solution to poverty is to abolish it directly by a now widely discussed measure: the guaranteed income. ... We are likely to find that the problems of housing and education, instead of preceding the elimination of poverty, will themselves be affected if poverty is first abolished.

Martin Luther King Jr.

4

Our World

Our world is in trouble. Every day brings more news of wars, terrorism, global warming, pollution, crimes, rising health care costs, layoffs, and other problems and threats.

Our government is failing us. It's mostly paralyzed by partisan disputes between Democrats and Republicans, by polarizing rhetoric from conservatives and liberals, by news reports that oversimplify issues and ignore the context, by the personal ambitions of elected officials and political appointees, by special interests lobbying to protect their profits and privileges. Our government is upholding the status quo by default and by design.

We individuals, almost all of us, have been abdicating our responsibilities as citizens. Instead of demanding real reforms and progress, we've been complaining and criticizing but mostly just hoping for change to come, somehow, from government or the market. We appear to have forgotten that we, together, are sovereign; that We the People create our government; that we are responsible for our government; that, consequently and truly, we are our government. We are the market, too.

Citizen Policies will provide each of us with regular reminders of our responsibility and our authority. Each of us, as well, will have added means to act responsibly and assert our authority.

Imagine that you are getting an extra $800 each month and performing some regular community service. So are your spouse and other adult family members. And your friends, your neighbors, their neighbors, and every other adult citizen.

What do you think that might mean for you and your family?

What might that do for your neighborhood and community? Your town or city? Your state? Our nation?

What might that do for our world?

5

Poverty

We can end debilitating poverty, hunger, and homelessness by enacting Citizen Policies. That's not happening with current policies, and appears impossible. Have you heard any elected official present a specific plan to end hunger or homelessness?

Providing for the poor is a moral and religious duty according to Christian, Jewish, Muslim, and many other traditions. Religious Americans, and secular humanists, too, might call for Citizen Policies as an expression of our values.

Relative poverty will persist, of course. There will still be people who earn or inherit more money, or save and invest more successfully. There will still be people who become poor following job loss, divorce, serious illness, or a natural disaster. Yet there will also be an absolute monetary safety net. Every citizen, regardless of personal circumstances, will have a basic income for food and shelter.

Still, too, some people will need extra help, at least occasionally. Examples are people with problems involving mental health or substance abuse. Assistance in such cases might come primarily from family members, friends, and neighbors performing Citizen Service. Religious or secular charities might facilitate or coordinate our Citizen Service. Government can act as a charity of last resort.

The economic playing field will be more level. Those of us who play fair and work hard will have more opportunities than today, and better opportunities, with better chances for success. Those who don't succeed will still be on the field, in the game, able to try again. Providing opportunities — that's what America is renowned for, what our government is supposed to do for us.

Politicians talk about providing economic opportunities. Their rhetoric is out of touch with our reality. Do you know any hard-working poor or middle-class person who has gotten rich? There are a few, of course — some professional athletes and entertainers, for example. There are also people who win the lottery. What are the odds? Anyone you know?

Education is supposed to be the best path out of poverty. It may be, though it's mostly for the next generation. In order to go to school, people need money for food, shelter, and tuition. Citizen Dividends will ensure that everyone who wants more education will be able to get it.

Our government declared a "war on poverty" in 1964. We lost. Surrendered unconditionally. We never even tried the guaranteed income strategy that was advocated by economists, CEOs, union leaders, moderate politicians, prominent newspapers, and a majority of ordinary people. The defeat of Nixon's Family Assistance Plan was a huge victory for the special interests.

The government program that has done by far the most good for the poor is the Earned Income Tax Credit. It was created in 1975, a vestige of the Family Assistance Plan, and expanded in 1993. The EITC gives extra cash to 24 million families with incomes of less than $40,000. But it has serious flaws. It provides no assistance at all to those who need it most, the very poor, because they do not earn enough to pay income taxes. It traps recipients in near-poverty, because the credit stops abruptly when people earn more than the cutoff amount. And, because it's a complicated part of the income tax code, millions of people don't get it even though they're eligible.

Citizen Dividends will be far more helpful than the EITC, a higher minimum wage, a living wage, tax cuts, tax credits, job programs, food stamps, unemployment compensation, microcredit, education subsidies, or any other policy or combination of policies. Some existing programs and policies may still be useful; many will not, and we'll be able to eliminate them.

Citizen Dividends will be better in another way, too. They won't just help the poor. They're for everyone. Programs for the poor are the first to be cut when politicians want to reduce government spending. Poor people can't afford lawyers and lobbyists. The poor depend on other people's political clout and goodwill. With Citizen Policies, we'll be helping the poor and ourselves, aligning our self-interest with our moral and religious values. We'll also be reinforcing our moral and religious values, and our political values, by treating everyone as equals, with dignity.

6

Crime

Picture a criminal.

When thinking about crime and criminals, most of us cue up some stereotype: a young black or Latino man from an inner-city neighborhood where unemployment is high, gangs are active, guns and drugs are easy to get, and there's plenty of money in the hands of thugs, pimps, and drug dealers. Is that what you saw?

Imagine Citizen Policies and the same young man. If he's not yet 18, he looks forward to receiving Citizen Dividends. If he's over 18, he has some income for food and shelter, guaranteed, as long as he obeys the law. There are jobs for him and his friends, because people are spending their Citizen Dividends at local stores, creating jobs. His parents, aunts, uncles, and other adults perform Citizen Service, perhaps assisting the police in solving crimes, perhaps helping young people stay in school, perhaps coaching or mentoring or tutoring.

Take these speculations a step further, and picture yourself in the young man's situation. With things as they are today, might you be tempted by crime? If you could not get into college or could not afford it, were not talented enough to become an entertainer, not strong enough or fast enough for pro sports, with no other way to earn more than the minimum wage, might you be tempted? Consider how you would feel, think, and act if we had Citizen Policies. If you were that young man, would it be easier to stay out of trouble? Would you be more likely to pursue legal ways to get ahead? Think about it.

Have you ever been the victim of a crime? If so, recall what happened — the incident, the aftermath, and the perpetrator, if known. What happened?

Suppose we already had Citizen Policies. What if the perpetrator had some guaranteed income? Do you think the crime would have occurred? Does it seem as if the police and justice system might have been more effective? Might the outcome have been more satisfying?

There are other types of crime, of course, including white-collar or corporate crimes — fraud, bribery, identity theft, and insider stock trading. A stereotype in those cases is a white man, superficially successful yet still greedy. Would Citizen Policies have an effect on Ken Lay, Jack Abramoff, Randy Cunningham, Bernie Ebbers, Dennis Kozlowski, or others like them? There's no way to know. Even so, it makes sense to expect a decline in corporate crime. Forget about the corporate criminal for a moment. Instead, think about people who work for him, people more like you. Currently, if you found out that your boss was a crook, would you blow the whistle? Knowing that you might be fired, would you report it to upper management, the FBI or Securities and Exchange Commission, or the media? If you had guaranteed economic security, would you be more likely to take the risk and do what's right? Yes? Does it make sense that other people would do the same?

Citizen Policies, in addition, will reduce the costs of crime by facilitating reform of the criminal justice system. Since 1980, the number of people in prison has more than quadrupled — and not because crime rates have risen steadily. They haven't. Many politicians, to show they're "tough on crime," call for longer sentences and mandatory minimums. Another factor is the political power of the prison industry. Building and running prisons creates lots of jobs, and lobbyists for the industry tout those jobs and contribute to political campaigns. Prisons are typically located where jobs are scarce, in poor, rural communities. Elected officials therefore have many incentives to spend our money to build prisons and keep them full.

Enacting Citizen Policies – especially if crime rates decline, which is nearly certain – will provide a good opportunity to reevaluate laws and sentences. We're spending many billions of dollars a year to incarcerate elderly prisoners who have high and rising medical costs. We're spending many billions to prosecute and incarcerate people for prostitution, possession of marijuana, and other nonviolent crimes. Is that necessary? Victimless acts might be decriminalized. There could be more use of electronic monitoring, community-based sentencing, and other alternative arrangements. Such reforms would be more just and more humane. And we'll save a lot of our taxpayer dollars.

Courts could redirect Citizen Dividends to pay fines, penalties, court costs, victim restitution, and other expenses associated with the crime or the justice system. People might perform Citizen Service to help rehabilitate prisoners and former prisoners, for example, by teaching inmates and ex-convicts to read, use computers, and find good jobs. The criminal justice system can become simpler, more cost-effective, more rational, and more humane — if that's what We the People want and demand.

7

Health Care

If you had an extra $800 a month, guaranteed, would you sleep better, eat better, have less stress? Do you think you'd be healthier? Would you upgrade your medical insurance to a more comprehensive plan? Would you buy insurance if you don't have any?

Currently, many of us can't afford to eat well or take the time to exercise regularly. Many of us can't afford to take good care of ourselves and the people we love. Stress is a fact of life, especially for the tens of millions of us who are living from paycheck to paycheck, at risk of losing our jobs, burdened by credit card debt, without medical insurance. And stress is a factor in heart disease, obesity, chronic pain, cancer, and countless other health conditions.

A guaranteed economic safety net that empowers individuals to look after their own health will mean lower health care costs for our society. Cutting costs is the first step in any serious approach to health care reform.

The health care system is in crisis, and everyone knows it. Costs are rising faster than the rate of inflation. More than 46 million Americans have no medical insurance. Additional tens of millions of us worry that our coverage is inadequate, that the company could refuse to pay for some necessary treatment. Tens of millions of us worry about losing our insurance if our employers relocate or declare bankruptcy. Employer-based insurance is an enormous burden on American companies, which are competing with companies in countries that provide national health care. The Medicare trust fund is running out of money. Medicaid is a significant drain on state governments.

Should we have universal health care, something like Medicare-for-all? Government mandates that individuals buy insurance, or employers provide it? Expanded health savings accounts, perhaps with refundable tax credits for poor people? More strict regulation of insurance companies, the hospital industry, and the pharmaceutical industry?

It will be a lot easier to debate these questions after we enact Citizen Policies. Everyone will have extra income that we can spend on health care. Many of us will be healthier. The need for reform will be less urgent, giving us opportunities to try different reforms at the state level. And everyone will be able to participate in the debates, making it possible for We the People to assert our sovereignty over the special interests. After half a century of failed reforms, Citizen Policies could be the key to fixing the broken health care system.

Here's another reason to enact Citizen Policies promptly: avian flu. Another: staph infections. Another: drug resistant tuberculosis. Some type of pandemic is inevitable, according to scientists at the Centers for Disease Control and Prevention. We have to be prepared. A quarantine might be necessary, closing airports, subways, shopping malls, and other public facilities. What about the people who work or shop in such places, or commute through them? A quarantine could last several weeks, even months. How will that affect you and your family? How will you manage? Containing a pandemic will require everyone's cooperation. Citizen Dividends will make it possible for all of us to act responsibly — and could thereby prevent social, economic, and political chaos.

8

Education

Do you have children? Grandchildren? Are you satisfied with the education they're getting? Are they, in your opinion, acquiring the knowledge and skills they'll need to succeed as adults?

Education is a high priority for most Americans, not just parents. That makes sense. Children, after all, will become voters, voting on issues that affect everyone. They'll also be workers, taxpayers, property owners, investors, and jurors. Educated voters and workers are essential for a healthy, prosperous, democratic, and compassionate society.

How can we improve our education system? Charter schools? Vouchers? Home-schooling? Require – or ban – specific texts, methods, or curricula? Routine testing of every student, as mandated by the No Child Left Behind law? Contract with private companies to provide schooling? Each approach has passionate supporters and opponents.

On one point, though, there is a strong consensus: Parents have to spend more time with their children. Parents are expected to be available for reading to young ones, meeting with teachers, helping with homework, supervising computer use, attending events at school. Citizen Dividends will make it easier for parents to afford the time.

Politicians tell us that they trust parents, they respect parents, they want parents to be actively involved in educating their children. Do you know any politician who doesn't say that? When parents are not involved, however, it's usually because they're busy working to earn money. Right? Politicians who are sincere about trusting parents, and sincerely committed to improving education, might recognize Citizen Dividends as the key to substantial parental involvement.

Just about every child occasionally needs extra, individual attention. They'll get extra attention, assistance, and mentoring from adults performing Citizen Service in the classroom. Classroom volunteers will provide many of the benefits of smaller class sizes without the added cost.

Parents who volunteer in classrooms, in addition, will be learning how to guide and assist their children more effectively at home. They'll also be learning about the teacher, curriculum, principal, educational philosophy, and school resources. Informed parents will be more responsible voters on education issues. Plus, when parents are volunteering in the schools, teachers will know the parents. That could aid teachers in giving children more appropriate individualized attention.

Citizen Dividends will also help families pay for higher education. Poor people will attain that entry into a middle-class life. Working families will be able to send their kids to college without incurring crushing debts.

Education does not stop with college, of course. Are there programs that would help you seek a better job? Continuing education that could advance your career? Classes you'd like to take for personal improvement? For fun? Education will be more available and affordable for everyone, at every age, for any reason, when we have Citizen Dividends.

9

Social Security

How can we save Social Security? Should we raise the retirement age? Increase payroll taxes? Supplement payroll taxes with funds from some other tax, perhaps on fossil fuels? Make 401(k) accounts available to all workers? Divert some of the trust fund into private accounts, which people control and invest for themselves? Let people control and invest all of their retirement money?

Each approach has special interests in opposite sides. Each special interest has elaborate economic projections and statistics to support some preferred plan. Most of us don't have time to figure it out. But we have to figure it out. The stakes are high. The choices are critical. Do the wrong thing, and some of us or many of us – perhaps you, your parents, or your children – could be destitute in later years.

Here's a better initial question: How can we ensure financial security for the elderly?

Citizen Dividends may be the simplest answer. It could also be the key to resolving our differences and reaching a consensus about Social Security.

That question – How can we ensure financial security for the elderly? – inspired Thomas Paine's proposal to give everyone age 50 or older a small sum each year. The same question provoked Francis Townsend, a family physician in Long Beach, Calif., to devise a plan to provide "liberal financial retirement for the aged" — a guaranteed income of $200 a month for everyone age 60 or older. (That was in 1934. The equivalent amount in today's dollars is about $2,800.) In the 18 months after Townsend published a small booklet with his plan, roughly two million Americans joined the movement to enact it. Their campaign, the Townsend Plan movement, led to winning Social Security in the first place.

If we start by updating Paine's and Townsend's insights and enacting Citizen Policies, every senior citizen will be more secure financially than today. Economic security will be guaranteed for our grandparents and parents, ourselves, our children and grandchildren and great-grandchildren.

After we do that, it might make sense to privatize Social Security partly or even completely. Or to raise the retirement age. Or to abolish the earnings cap. Or to create universal 401(k)s. Or to supplement the trust fund with higher taxes on fossil fuels. Or to do something no one has yet thought of. Whatever we do and whenever we do it, everyone will have a secure income while we consider the options.

10

Family Values

Politicians, pundits, and preachers have a lot to say about "family values." Religious conservatives use the phrase as a code for opposing abortion, banning same-sex marriage, insisting on abstinence-only sex education. Some liberals turn the phrase around and talk about "valuing families" by, for example, requiring companies to give workers time off to care for their young children.

Such rhetoric can be a distraction, an added burden, or worse, a form of coercion and cause of shame or guilt. Parents need a break, not slogans or lectures. Parents need what Citizen Dividends will provide: more income and economic security.

What does "family values" mean to you?

More to the point: What are *your* family values? What are your values for your family, especially for your children?

Family values – regardless of how you use that term – are learned and shared and solidified through the time families spend together, the things families do together. With Citizen Policies, you and your spouse will be more able to live

according to your values. And to live your values in the way
you raise and educate your children.

- You and your family will be able to devote more time
  to activities that express your values.

- You'll have added income for education, faith-based
  pursuits, and other value-oriented activities.

- You'll be able to contribute more money to people
  and organizations that share your values and are
  working to fulfill them.

- For your Citizen Service, you and your spouse might
  volunteer in your children's school or afterschool
  program or church group. That will provide further
  opportunities for you to be involved with your
  children, their educations, and their values.

Talk about family values is particularly loud and lively
after incidents of children using guns. Liberals blame the
gun culture. Conservatives point fingers at the Internet, hip-
hop music, or other elements of popular culture. But neither
guns nor popular culture lead to trouble when parents are
present and actively engaged in parenting. Many parents,
though, can't afford to be present; they're busy working to
earn enough money to pay their bills. Perhaps the most
effective way to prevent children from misusing guns – and
to keep all of our children safe – is to provide parents, all
parents, with extra income.

Within families, typically, worries and conflicts about
money are a common cause of stress. There's never "enough"
money. Monetary stresses are a factor in many cases of child

abuse, spousal abuse, suicide, and homicide. Such incidents are likely to decline significantly when every adult has real economic security. Spouses who are abused or feel threatened will have their own safety net to use in seeking another environment for themselves and their children.

Citizen Policies will promote strong marriages and family values in another way as well. Young adults don't earn much money. Many are paying college loans. The joys of new marriages and children are often spoiled by monetary stress, which can cause marriages to fail and children to suffer. Extra income will make young families more stable and secure. Parents will be more able to cope when children are sick or schools are closed due to snow or other emergencies. It will be easier for people to be full-time parents, if that's what they want. Young families will therefore be more likely to mature and thrive — and to succeed in raising healthy children.

The strongest, happiest, and most enduring marriages are those in which the couple share a real sense of partnership. Sharing and partnership will be encouraged by the inherent equality of Citizen Policies.

For families and individuals to be healthy and happy, an essential value is optimism — and realistic hope for a better, brighter, more prosperous future. Citizen Policies will provide reasons for hope. Everyone will have reasons to be confident that life will be better for our children and grandchildren.

11

Racism and Discrimination

Some form of universal economic security is a prerequisite for ending racism, discrimination, and related problems. Those among us who have been victims of discrimination, after all, are often poor, impoverished by the discrimination. Many victims can't afford to pursue justice. Earning money for food and shelter normally, sensibly, has to come first.

Citizen Policies will ensure that every adult citizen has real economic security. *Every* adult citizen, regardless of race, age, class, gender, ethnic background, sexual orientation, appearance, physical abilities, or other differences. There will be a new baseline of economic justice and economic equality. Each of us will consequently be on the political and legal playing fields.

It's relatively easy to protect existing privileges, and hard to challenge injustice. That's partly because the status quo is familiar. We are accustomed to the existing system of power and privileges. We take it for granted, and generally know how it operates and what to expect. We are consequently biased in favor of the status quo and often not aware of that bias. Progress takes time. Preexisting habits and prejudices often recur. And progress can provoke a backlash, particularly when people are discomforted or inconvenienced by the progress. Economic security will help everyone be more comfortable as change occurs.

The power of Citizen Policies to facilitate lasting progress is most evident in the ongoing debates about immigration. Immigrants come to this country looking for jobs. Current workers are afraid of losing their jobs, afraid immigrants will "take" their jobs. Employers have to earn some profit, at least enough to stay in business; they therefore seek to keep wages low, and to hire the cheapest labor they can. Right? Isn't that what we hear from people on all sides of these issues? Immigrants, American workers, and employers are pursuing self-interests. Everyone is concerned about money and the means to survive.

Are you a citizen? Suppose you're getting an extra $800 each month, independent of your job. And the extra income is guaranteed, unconditional. Would you be more secure? Would you be less afraid of losing your job? Think about it. You could invest your Citizen Dividends to learn the skills to qualify for a better job. You could start your own business. You could afford to move somewhere that offers more opportunities. You could afford to accept lower wages or a shorter work week or earlier retirement. With these added choices and reduced monetary stresses, might you be more comfortable with immigrants? Might you feel more empathy for them and their situation?

Are you an immigrant, not a citizen but eligible to become one? Would you be more eager to become a citizen, knowing that it will mean extra income?

Are you an immigrant, but not eligible for citizenship, perhaps because you entered the United States illegally? Are you content with undocumented status and a low-wage job? You might simply accept things as they are. You could go back to your home country and apply to return legally. You could also start a movement in your home country for some type of guaranteed basic income. That would let you and your family members – and your friends, neighbors, and so on – achieve some economic security without leaving and trying to get into the United States.

For citizens and noncitizens, for immigrants who came legally or illegally, Citizen Policies will help us reduce tensions, resolve conflicts, and focus on creating better conditions for everyone.

The power of this approach to racism is three-fold. First, it works with and through individuals — you, your family members, your neighbors, and others. Unique individuals. Second, this approach is unconditional and universal. Every individual citizen will benefit equally. Every citizen will be treated with equal respect and dignity. Third, this approach orients us toward the present and the future.

Current efforts mostly overlook individuals. They operate instead by grouping people into categories: blacks, Latinos, gays, and so on. Categories are analyzed statistically and compared with other categories, typically whites or "the middle class." Then the statistics provide the basis for proposed remedies. Categories and statistics, though, are abstractions. "Racism" and "discrimination" are abstractions. It's impossible to eliminate an abstraction. Citizen Policies treat every adult citizen as an individual.

Current efforts are conditional. Even worse, the conditions are divisive; they're based on race or some other category. The conditions and categories distract us from both our individuality and our common humanity. Conditional programs, moreover, produce further divisions and potential conflicts, dividing the few beneficiaries from everyone else. For those who benefit – from affirmative action, for example – there is often a stigma attached: maybe they weren't really the best qualified, maybe someone else lost a job because of a quota system. Benefits paid equally to everyone carry no such stigma.

Attempts to end racism and discrimination typically get bogged down in debates about the past. A lot of effort is spent revisiting injustices that happened decades or generations ago. The focus on the past can stir up old resentments and upsets, distracting everyone from today's issues and delaying progress. Every delay compounds the injustices.

Progress depends on how we treat each other. As individuals. Today. When each of us knows that he or she can afford food and shelter regardless of what others say or do – and regardless of any past discrimination or perception of discrimination – it will be easier for us to be respectful and mutually accountable. It will be easier for everyone to act with dignity and to respect one another's dignity.

Mutual respect is especially important for progress on longstanding issues. Many of us ignore questions about reparations for slavery and the exploitation of Native Americans. Many of us dismiss these issues as impossibly complicated matters of history. Yet historical wrongs continue to have unjust consequences. With mutual respect and a sincere commitment to justice, we can achieve resolutions that are reasonable and fair.

Seeking justice and pursuing it is a moral and religious duty. Citizen Policies will help each of us engage in that pursuit.

12

Pollution and Global Warming

We can slow the rate of climate change. We can restore our environment. It's not too late — not quite. We can do it, moreover, with minimal government interference in our lives and businesses.

First we need Citizen Dividends. Then we have to consider something elected officials are not talking about: the fact that our government pays huge subsidies to the fossil fuel industries. Those subsidies promote the burning of oil, coal, and natural gas. Our government, which should be working to reverse global warming, is using our taxpayer dollars to accelerate it. That's insane. We have to eliminate the subsidies.

Eliminating subsidies will mean higher prices. That's why we start with Citizen Dividends. Everyone will have extra income and economic security as we adapt.

Imagine that you're getting an extra $800 each month. Imagine also that prices are higher for gasoline, electricity, transportation, and heating your home. And that you know prices will go up even more. What would you do? How might that affect your life choices?

You could move to a smaller home closer to where you work. Find a job closer to where you live. Telecommute a few days a week. Quit your job and start a home-based business. Add insulation to your home. Buy a hybrid car. Use mass transit or a bicycle. Vacation near your home or by train, instead of flying to some tropical island. Each of us and all of us will have added means and incentives to do what's best for ourselves and our planet.

Yes, some people really like their SUVs and their big houses in distant suburbs, and they'll spend their Citizen Dividends to maintain that lifestyle. At least the rest of us will no longer be subsidizing their lifestyle choices. Most such people will eventually get tired of paying the high prices. Or they'll get tired of being nagged by their children and grandchildren about global warming, energy conservation, and their responsibility for our planet.

As you do what's best for yourself and your family – as all of us do what's best for ourselves and our families – rapid progress will come from the sum of our individual choices. That's "the market." The auto industry, home builders, appliance manufactures, and other businesses and industries will supply more energy-efficient goods, services, and technology, responding to demands from customers and citizens. Supply and demand. The market.

Conservative Republicans say we should trust the market to solve our problems. Subsidies distort the market. Will conservatives support an end to the subsidies? Liberal Democrats say we need government programs and regulations, including strict efficiency standards for cars, homes, and appliances, plus subsidies for alternative fuels. Will liberals admit that such programs are inadequate, and might be unnecessary?

Politicians from the left and the right assert, with lots of supporting evidence, that we Americans demand low prices for gasoline, electricity, and just about everything else. Will we consent to higher fuel prices? Will we concede the truth that higher prices can be good for us, good for our communities, our nation, and our planet? Maybe — once we're cushioned from the effects of higher prices, once each of us has the means to adapt as we choose.

Oil company profits are many billions of dollars each year. We're giving them more billions of dollars a year from our public treasury. Direct and indirect subsidies include exempting companies from environmental regulations; paying for research into getting fuel from tar sands, oil shale, and "clean" coal; giving tax credits to businesses for utility bills and to individuals for mortgage interest on large homes; building or expanding airports and encouraging air travel; failing to tax fossil fuel companies for pollution-caused diseases, such as asthma, emphysema, and cancer; charging inadequate royalties for drilling and mining on land that We the People own through our government. In addition, we indirectly subsidize the oil companies through military spending to protect "our" supplies of foreign oil.

Subsidies have been government policy for decades, under Democrats and Republicans. Perhaps that made sense once upon a time. No longer. We have to reduce our use of fossil fuels, not subsidize it.

ExxonMobil, Chevron, et. al., will still explore and drill for oil and natural gas, and will still build pipelines and operate refineries. Those activities will still be profitable, after all. The notion that ending subsidies will cause shortages is oil company propaganda. Indeed, when the companies are no longer profiting so greatly from our subsidies, they'll have to focus on their core energy businesses; they might therefore be more eager to provide alternative fuels and promote energy efficiency. Subsidies continue because of the political power of the oil companies and the corruption of our government. And because we individuals and We the People have been shortsighted and foolish.

The conventional rationale for subsidizing fossil fuel production and use, as with many other policies, is that the subsidies create jobs. Those jobs, however, are in businesses and industries that are adding to pollution and global warming, and the jobs will disappear sooner or later. Eliminating the subsidies will also create jobs — sustainable jobs, and probably more of them. There will be lots of new jobs in businesses that promote conservation, efficiency, alternative energy sources, and new technology; those are the jobs of the future.

Climate change is happening. There will be more intense and destructive hurricanes, floods, droughts, and heat waves. That means there will be occasional shortages of food, clean water, and electricity, with higher and less stable prices for these necessities. Many of us will have to relocate our homes, jobs, and businesses. Companies and whole industries will become obsolete. New businesses and industries will have to emerge.

Everyone will be affected in many ways, unpredictably. We're going to have to adapt. Citizen Policies will help each of us adapt appropriately, skillfully, quickly — ideally before some crisis catches us unprepared. Regardless of what happens, each of us will know that we can afford food and shelter. We won't have to worry so much about paying the bills next month. That will allow us to focus more on next year, the next decade, and beyond, to focus on our grandchildren and great-grandchildren and the world they will inhabit.

Where do you live? Is it an area that's subject to hurricanes? Floods? Droughts?

Are you preparing for climate change?

Where does your food come from? What about your water and electricity? Do you have a backup plan?

What do you expect our world to be like for your children and grandchildren?

These are serious questions that each of us ought to be thinking about. Climate change is accelerating. Those of us who fail to prepare will be hurt much more than those who act wisely. That's one of the lessons of Hurricane Katrina. It's clear that our government has not learned, at least not yet. What about you? Did you learn? Are you preparing?

Eliminating subsidies to the fossil fuel companies will do much more than slow the rate of climate change. Every form of pollution – the mercury and toxic chemicals in our streams, the litter on the streets of our towns and cities, the smoke and bad smells in our air, and so on – is at least partly a product of fossil fuel consumption. Eliminating subsidies will immediately reduce the pollution of our air, water, and land.

With higher fossil fuel prices:

- Wind, solar, biomass, and other sustainable energy sources will be more cost-effective.

- Our towns and cities will be more enjoyable and attractive, with fewer traffic jams, less suburban sprawl, and maybe also better mass transit.

- More farmers will switch to organic methods, away from synthetic fertilizers and pesticides; organic food will be more available and affordable.

- Scientists and engineers will develop plastics, building materials, and other stuff from plants; new plastics will be biodegradable and economical to recycle.

- Manufacturers will find more uses for recycled materials, and will pay more money for them.

This progress, moreover, will be realized through the market, with minimal government regulations or mandates.

There is one thing our government ought to do. Progress will be more rapid and reliable if fuel prices are relatively stable and predictable. As we've seen repeatedly since the 1960s, fluctuating prices, including falling prices, cause widespread economic and political disruptions. Falling prices also reinforce the delusion that we don't have to conserve. The primary beneficiaries of fluctuating prices are financial speculators. Our government can stabilize prices by implementing a floating tax at the wholesale level, when the fuel first enters the economic stream at the port, mine, or well-head. That will help individuals, families, and businesses plan and budget.

As we in the United States reduce our consumption of fossil fuels, prices will decline worldwide. That means people in China and other countries could take advantage of the lower prices, burn more fuel, and offset progress. But the Chinese people and their government know it's in their interest to reduce fuel consumption. Already, for example, China has much stricter auto fuel efficiency standards than we do, and their government is investing heavily in alternative energy. There's no evidence to support any suggestion that they'll backtrack.

Regardless of what other countries do, we have to act. We Americans consume roughly 25 percent of the world's fossil fuels and produce 25 percent of greenhouse gases, even though we are just 5 percent of the world's population. The faster we act and the more we do, the better it will be for our planet, our nation, and each of us individuals. Plus, We the People and our government will be able – sincerely, not hypocritically – to encourage conservation in China, India, and elsewhere. And American companies will develop more efficient products and technologies that they can sell in other countries.

Will enacting Citizen Policies, eliminating fossil fuel subsidies, and stabilizing fuel prices be sufficient? Will consumption decline fast enough to prevent the catastrophic changes that scientists are predicting? There's no way to know. If more ambitious reductions are required, Citizen Policies will ease the way politically toward further action. We could enact a "carbon tax" based on the amount of carbon released when any fossil fuel is burned. It would be necessary, probably, to increase the carbon tax periodically — and we could increase Citizen Dividends at the same time.

Another approach is a "cap-and-trade" program for carbon dioxide. Our government would limit the total quantity of emissions and sell permits to emit shares of the total. Companies that reduce emissions – with new technology, say – could trade or sell their permits to other companies. Cap-and-trade would create a market for pollution permits, rewarding companies that innovate and penalizing companies that don't. The incentives would increase as the caps become tighter, which should happen every year. Making the caps tighter, in addition, would increase revenues from permit sales. The money earned would pay for enforcement — and help pay for higher Citizen Dividends.

Special interests, if they cannot block reform completely, will work to delay and minimize it. With cap-and-trade, they'll want the caps to be relatively high, unchanging, and based on current emissions. Citizen Policies will help us thwart the special interests and their tactics.

Even with such programs in place, individual action will be essential. You and other individuals might invest your Citizen Dividends on education, learning how to live more sustainably. Or start businesses or careers that enhance sustainability. You might contribute some of your Citizen Service time – or some of your extra income – to groups that are recycling, planting trees, protecting endangered species, conserving land from development, starting trusts for public land and other resources, educating people about ecology and sustainability, or taking legal or political actions against polluters.

Probably the most important thing you can do – and something everyone who cares about these issues ought to do, starting right away – is get more involved in politics. Just about every Democratic and Republican elected official has taken contributions from fossil fuel companies, auto manufacturers, real estate developers, and related special interests. We the People have to assert our sovereignty over those special interests and the politicians who work for them.

13

Farms, Forests, and Wetlands

In political discussions about farms, forests, and wetlands – whether to preserve them and how to preserve them, whether to allow development and what kind of development – we often hear that it's a matter of "the economy versus the environment." We hear the same phrase when people talk about pollution, climate change, endangered species, mining, logging, road-building, and related issues. The familiar phrase sounds reasonable and sensible. But think about it. Are the economy and the environment really conflicting interests? How can that be?

People who talk about "the economy versus the environment" are usually calling for more economic growth, more jobs. Our first priority, they tell us, has to be the economy. Preserving habitats and species is a luxury; creating jobs is a necessity. Creating jobs, also, according to politicians, CEOs, and real estate developers, will increase economic growth and provide tax revenues to pay for environmental protection.

Citizen Dividends will take the jobs card out of politicians' hands. Political discourse won't be constrained by any presumed imperative to create jobs. Everyone will have some income and economic security independent of any job. It will consequently be easier for all of us – even CEOs and real estate developers, even politicians – to appreciate the fact that forests, wetlands, and endangered species are valuable public assets. We humans need a healthy environment. That includes farms, gardens, and parks in urban areas; farms and gardens, after all, are the source of our food. We also need, literally and absolutely *need*, the fresh air and clean water we get from natural processes in forests and wetlands.

Do you enjoy views of open spaces, lakes and rivers, wild animals, butterflies, flocks of birds, and other natural phenomena? Do you like to listen to the birds and smell the flowers? Do you prefer fresh, locally grown vegetables, fruits, and other foods? Are you concerned about the nutritional quality of foods that come from thousands of miles away?

Do you want your grandchildren to have similar experiences of nature?

Decisions about these issues are being made every day by local governments. But political practices are corrupted by campaign contributions from industries that profit from development. Those special interests include home builders, real estate speculators, highway construction companies, and financial institutions.

We have to demand that government serve our interests, We the People, not the elite special interests. We have to demand an end to corporate subsidies and campaign finance corruption. We have to demand political recognition of future generations and the intrinsic value of nature. Citizen Policies will enhance our ability to make those demands effectively, without special interests changing the subject.

14

Local Communities

Think about where you live. What do you suppose Citizen Policies might mean for your neighborhood, your community? Can you envision changes you would like? Could there be fewer things you dislike? If you would rather be living somewhere else, think about where you want to be. Might you use the extra income to move and get resettled? Can you envision enhancements to your new community?

In big cities, small towns, and the suburbs in between, local businesses will thrive from people spending their Citizen Dividends. Local businesses, in addition, will gain competitive advantages relative to Wal-Mart, Home Depot, and other out-of-town chains. That's because the large companies benefit disproportionately from subsidies to create jobs and promote foreign trade; we'll be eliminating those subsidies. As economic conditions change, moreover, small businesses will be able to adapt more rapidly and appropriately than large retail chains.

With nearly everyone engaged in Citizen Service, local communities will be more attractive, safer, and more enjoyable for you, your family, and your friends. Local schools will benefit from parents and other adults doing Citizen Service in classrooms and PTAs. Schools will also be better funded, probably, because people will have Citizen Dividends and might be more willing to support local school bonds. In addition, there are likely to be more local events – theater, music, parades, book discussion groups, and such – with more participants and larger audiences. That will mean new opportunities for you to meet your neighbors and possibly become friends.

In big cities around the country, poor African-American and Latino residents are being displaced by wealthier people moving in from the suburbs in a process of gentrification. With Citizen Dividends, current residents will become the gentry, with extra income so they can afford to stay as urban communities are restored and improved.

In small towns, many of which have lost population in recent decades, people will return to take advantage of the low cost of living. Small towns and rural areas will be revitalized economically and culturally. Suburban communities will become more distinct, unique, and attractive.

Progress everywhere will be the result of individual decisions and market-based activities. We won't have to wait or depend on government programs. To appreciate how and why that will happen, imagine a real estate developer with millions of dollars to invest. Today, it is often a smart investment to buy land on the outskirts of a city and to build houses, a shopping mall, or an industrial park. Local governments subsidize such development by building roads, schools, and other infrastructure. (Elected officials like to build stuff; it's how they create jobs they can boast about when they run for reelection. Plus, they get campaign contributions from the developers, banks, and other industries that profit from building stuff.) Suburbs sprawl. Traffic gets worse. Downtown areas are left to deteriorate. Pollution increases. Wetlands are destroyed. Forests are cut down. Farmlands are lost, causing a decline in the freshness and quality of food for local residents. These changes are happening in towns and cities across the country.

Consider what the developer might do if we enact Citizen Policies and eliminate the subsidies. The smart investments, typically, will involve compact redevelopment within city limits. Those investments will therefore be favored by banks, pension funds, and other lenders. The developer might include mass transit, which increases property values significantly. Residents would be more likely to have a real voice in the planning, instead of being shut out while developers and politicians decide the details in some back room.

We can simultaneously reduce sprawl and traffic, revitalize rural small towns, and rebuild inner-city neighborhoods. We can do that, moreover, with minimal assistance from our federal or state governments.

15

National Security

Since September 11, 2001, we've heard a lot of talk about terrorism, war, and national security. Everything changed that day, people say. Even so, government officials told us to get on with our lives as before, to go to work and go shopping.

We are urged to do one thing differently: be vigilant. When government officials tell us that – and they do so every time there's a specific terrorist threat – they ignore the fact that we're busy. Many of us are being vigilant in search of a job, extra income, next month's rent. That vigilance is full-time work; looking for signs of terrorists is usually an afterthought, or less. Immediate self-interest is far more compelling than vague warnings.

Citizen Policies will make us safer. Fewer worries about economic security will enable everyone to pay closer attention to their surroundings and the world. Everyone will also have time to learn skills that will be valuable to their communities in an emergency, and to make plans and preparations for disasters.

Think about how much safer we'll be when, instead of just being told to be vigilant, we're taught how. As a form of Citizen

Service, we might be taught what to look for and what to do in the event of an emergency. There could be site-specific programs with local police. You and your family might learn first aid and other emergency skills alongside your neighbors. You might prepare with people where you work, or people you ride with on buses, subways, commuter trains.

As an added benefit of such preparations, you'll be getting to know your neighbors, co-workers, and co-commuters. That will make all of us more secure. When you know your neighbors, you'll also be better able to identify any stranger. You might introduce yourself to the stranger, inviting him or her to become more familiar. A stronger sense of community can be lifesaving in any emergency. Safety in numbers — right?

One of the lessons of September 11 is that ordinary people can do extraordinary heroic things. Sometimes it just takes common sense and an ability to remain calm during an emergency. It was ordinary people, armed only with information from their cell phones, who brought down the plane in Pennsylvania and prevented some far greater disaster in Washington, D.C. At the World Trade Center, ordinary people saved many lives by helping others get down the stairs and away from the buildings. Ordinary people joined in the rescues there and at the Pentagon.

Ordinary people demonstrated similar courage and compassion in New Orleans after Hurricane Katrina. Imagine how different that situation would have been if more residents were trained and prepared in advance. Think about how many lives might be saved in future hurricanes, floods, earthquakes, and other natural disasters. And in the event of any terrorist attack.

In any emergency, we depend on police, firefighters, medical providers, and the government officials who coordinate the first responders. The professionals will be more effective when the people who happen to be on the scene have had some training. Professional responders will be able to direct people to assist them appropriately. That might mean giving first aid; gathering requested supplies, like blankets or bandages; writing down the names and phone numbers of people who witnessed the event; keeping bystanders out of the way, while advising them what to do and where to go.

In our world of 7 billion people, there are sure to be many thousands or tens of thousands of would-be terrorists. There must be many tens of millions of sympathizers, who might provide a bit of assistance or simply look the other way. Some potential terrorists and sympathizers have grievances: U.S. forces in Iraq, Afghanistan, and Saudi Arabia; Guantanamo and Abu Ghraib; U.S. aid to Israel, and Israel's treatment of the Palestinian people; the many times the CIA acted to overthrow democratically elected governments, including Iran's in 1953; and, here at home, the incidents at Waco and Ruby Ridge. Some potential terrorists don't care about the facts — they just want to attack us because the United States is the one superpower, military, political, economic, and cultural. Some "terrorists" are really victims of untreated mental illness looking for a dramatic way to commit suicide.

Experts say it's almost impossible to stop a terrorist who's willing to die. Even one or two people can do enormous damage with a car bomb, portable missile, vial of toxic chemicals, or conventional bomb that contains some radioactive material. Information about how to obtain or construct such weapons is available on the Internet. The materials are cheap.

Our security as individuals and as a nation depends on everyone being vigilant. That's been confirmed in the years since September 11. In just about every arrest of suspected terrorists, every foiled terrorist plot, ordinary citizens performed key roles. Vigilant citizens and local law enforcement are our first line of defense.

The sooner we implement Citizen Policies, the safer we will be.

16

Globalization

Global free trade, we're told, provides jobs and economic growth that benefit everyone — a rising tide that lifts our rowboats along with the yachts. We consumers in the United States pay lower prices and gain access to more material goods, and more varied goods. People in poorer countries earn money by producing those goods.

Is your boat floating calmly? Are you enjoying the reputed benefits of globalization, a secure job, lower prices, and high-quality goods imported from other countries? Are you catching up to the yachts, perhaps about to climb aboard a luxury cruise ship? Or are you having to row harder and faster every day to stay afloat? Is your boat just a life raft? Are you sinking?

Many businesses are struggling to "compete in the global economy." That's a common reason companies give for closing facilities, laying off workers, moving production to Mexico or China or India. It's the reason they ask workers to accept lower wages or mandatory overtime. It's the reason they cut, abandon, or "restructure" health care and pension funds. It's the reason they demand tax breaks or other subsidies from local or state governments, or waivers from environmental regulations.

Have you ever been laid off? Have you been asked to work longer hours or for lower pay? Has your health care or pension been cut or modified? Have any of these things happened to your family members, friends, or neighbors?

What about your local government? Has it been bullied by some major employer into paying out a big chunk of your taxpayer dollars in subsidies?

With Citizen Policies, you and your family will have extra income that you can use to enjoy the benefits of global trade. You'll also be protected from the negative impact of globalization, and able to adapt more easily as economic conditions change.

Workers and communities will have more power to stop big companies from extorting us. If some major employer threatens to close a facility, workers could call their bluff. Workers could afford to go on strike indefinitely. Workers might organize to buy the facility, perhaps with funds from labor unions, credit unions, and local banks. Politicians will be more likely to favor the workers and other residents who vote, instead of the corporate executives and distant shareholders who only give campaign contributions.

"There is no alternative" to globalization, according to many Democratic and Republican leaders and their corporate backers. "It's good for America," they tell us, "good for the economy." Citizen Policies will ensure that each and all of us share some of that goodness.

These benefits can be just a first step. Starting with Citizen Policies in the United States, we can globalize democracy. We can globalize justice. We can globalize peace.

17

Other Countries

If Citizen Policies makes sense for us in the United States, what about for other countries?

Every country has unique problems, of course, and unique political conditions. Each will therefore have to devise its own version.

Brazil is already getting started. They learned about guaranteed income from us. In the late 1960s, when economists and politicians in the United States were debating Nixon's Family Assistance Plan, a young Brazilian student named Eduardo Matarazzo Suplicy was living in Michigan, working on a Ph.D. in economics. Dr. Suplicy returned to Sao Paulo to teach at the university, lecturing about guaranteed income and the Alaska Permanent Fund Dividend. He also became active in politics; was a cofounder of the Worker's Party, with Luis Inacio Lula da Silva; and, in 1992, was the first member of the party elected to the senate. Senator Suplicy proposed a law declaring that everyone has a right to a minimum income. The senate passed it unanimously in 2003. By the end of 2006, more than 11 million poor families were receiving cash grants, the "bolsa familia."

In Ireland, England, Finland, Australia, and other countries, basic income advocates are in national parliaments, even in governing coalitions. Advocates maintain that an unconditional basic income will provide a much more reliable social safety net than existing programs. In most of those countries, moreover, social programs are being cut; that's globalization, governments trying to compete with the United States and China.

Another country moving toward guaranteed basic income is South Africa. Millions of South Africans have no regular income. The only welfare program is for single mothers with children under age 7. In 2002, a government commission endorsed a plan to provide a monthly Basic Income Grant to everyone age 7 or older. The proposed BIG is 100 Rand, approximately $12 a month. It's just enough to ensure that people can afford to eat, making it possible for everyone to be productive at work and in school. The plan is extremely popular. Advocates include the South African Council of Churches; the Congress of South Africa Trade Unions; a diverse coalition of organizations working on poverty, AIDS, children's health, and women's issues; and Nobel Peace Prize Winner Archbishop Desmond Tutu. But not President Thabo Mbeki, who opposed it because it would mean raising taxes on the very rich.

In Mozambique, Prime Minister Pascoal Mocumbi announced in 2002 that his government wanted to introduce a BIG, but couldn't afford it. A basic income is a necessary step, he declared, toward providing health care and education. It "would provide vulnerable families with considerable room to maneuver in their survival strategies." Mozambique is even poorer than its neighbor, South Africa. Roughly 70 percent of Mozambican families live below the local poverty line. The government is highly indebted to the World Bank and International Monetary Fund.

Our government could assist Mozambique by directing the World Bank and IMF to fund its program. A BIG of, say, $12 a month for every adult would cost less than $1.5 billion a year. We could provide some of the money, and call on other wealthy countries to contribute. Funds might also come from the Gates Foundation and other private groups that are working in Africa to provide health care and other services. Three to five years ought to be enough time to see if people become healthier and more productive. If that happens, as seems certain, their government will be less dependent on international aid. They might in time become self-sufficient.

What do you think? Have you read or heard anything else that offers real hope for people in extremely poor countries?

Currently, foreign aid mostly goes to government banks, even where politicians are known to be corrupt or unreliable. Some of our "foreign aid" is specifically earmarked for purchases from U.S. companies that pay U.S. citizens' salaries. Some of our foreign aid is weapons and other military supplies. A major goal of aid, typically, is to create jobs. But very poor people in poor countries need food and shelter right away; it's cruel to insist that they wait, and unjust to make them dependent on potential employers who often provide unsafe or degrading jobs in unregulated conditions.

We could direct our government to offer aid through local Citizen Dividends. That would help countries create reliable banks, postal services, census bureaus, and other institutions — infrastructure that's a prerequisite for markets, economic growth, foreign investment, and democracy. Wherever politicians or central bankers appear to be corrupt, our aid might involve administering or supervising the program, hiring local people and training them. Even if we spend the same amount as we do today, the benefits will be vastly greater.

There are probably many countries that would like to try it. Haiti? The unrest there has been so great in recent decades that the U.S. military has intervened several times to restore order. Military interventions are extremely expensive. Mexico? This will do more than help the Mexican people and their government; we'll benefit, too. Among other things, Mexicans will have more income to buy stuff that's made in the United States, leading to a better balance of trade between our countries. They'll be more able and likely to clean up their environment, reducing air and water pollution that cross the border. And there will be fewer Mexicans trying to get into the United States; the main reason people come here, after all, is that they can't support themselves and their families.

You might think about these possibilities the next time you hear or read about immigration from Mexico, Guatemala, and other countries. And the next time you hear or read about political unrest in such countries. And about NAFTA, the trade deregulation pact between the United States, Mexico and Canada. Our government has sought for years to expand NAFTA to include countries in Central America and South America. Negotiations have stalled repeatedly over issues involving subsidies, environmental standards, worker rights, and immigration. Perhaps the key to enacting new trade agreements is to start with Citizen Dividends in the countries that want to join.

Why not encourage Mexicans to enact their own version of Citizen Dividends? Why not offer this type of aid to Haiti, and help them implement some program? Why not ask other wealthy countries, the United Nations, the World Bank, and the IMF to make it the preferred form of assistance to extremely poor countries?

Why not?

Current policies are not working for ordinary people in very poor countries. It makes sense to try something different.

18

World Peace

Is world peace something you think about? Something you dream about or pray for? Do you want our government to make peace a national priority?

World peace is possible. We Americans can lead the way by enacting Citizen Policies.

You can contribute significantly. You can help us achieve peace faster. You could thereby save countless lives.

There are many obstacles to peace. War is a big part of our lives, our culture. Tens of millions of us depend, directly or indirectly, on military spending. Special interests involved with the military and related industries are among the richest and most politically powerful.

War, threats of war, and preparations for war are very good for elected officials. Talking about the threats, promising to be tough, calling for more military spending, defining "patriotism" as unwavering support for a big military — these are proven effective ways to get votes. These are also good ways to get campaign contributions from special interests that profit from war. Tough-talking politicians who are not reelected can earn lots of money as lobbyists for the special interests. So, for elected officials, militarism is always a safe bet, with a nice payout regardless of what happens in the next election; pursuing peace takes real courage.

War is good for elected officials in another way, too. It keeps us busy waving flags and praying for our soldiers. Time for patriotism, people say, time to show our support, not the time for political reforms. Pundits and journalists are also busy, and eager to be seen as patriots who support our government.

War, therefore, is especially good for the president. Presidents use wars to enhance their power, prestige, and legacies, and turn our attention away from domestic policy failures. Enhancing the president's power and prestige, in addition, is good for the president's party. That's not just the politicians. Consultants, campaign contributors, allied pundits, and other supporters gain status and potential influence, and sometimes additional opportunities to earn money as lobbyists and TV commentators.

Presidents seem to be particularly disposed to lie to us about war. Lyndon Johnson and Richard Nixon did not tell us the truth about Vietnam. George W. Bush did not tell us the truth about Iraq. Even "Honest Abe" Lincoln invented reasons to lock political critics in jail during the Civil War.

Government officials, Democrats and Republicans, have said the war on terrorism will continue indefinitely. That means there will be U.S. forces in Iraq, Afghanistan, and dozens of other countries indefinitely. It means American citizens will have civil liberties curtailed indefinitely. Some officials have said the war on terrorism should be called "the long war."

As part of its strategy for fighting terrorism, our government is giving or selling weapons to authoritarian regimes, including Pakistan, Uzbekistan, Egypt, and Saudi Arabia. Those regimes are somewhat unstable. They will eventually collapse. The weapons might be sold to, given to, or stolen by terrorists who want to attack us.

Is our government arming potential terrorists? Could the weapons our government is sending to other countries be used one day against U.S. soldiers or civilians? Government officials say it won't happen. Of course they say that. They say whatever promotes their preferred policies. But their assertions defy logic and deny history. Throughout the 1980s, our government supported Saddam Hussein. Our government also provided weapons to the Afghani mujaheddin, which included Osama bin Laden and the Taliban.

Arming people who might someday attack us — that's one way to have a long war. It makes sense if the goal is to sell lots of weapons, burn lots of oil, generate lots of profit for the military industries, and give greater power to the president and other elected officials. Is that what We the People want? Are those our goals?

Current practices and policies do not lead toward peace. They make it unattainable. We're heading in the wrong direction. We have to assert our sovereignty and take back our government.

Think about Citizen Policies, what that will mean and make possible. When every citizen's economic security is guaranteed, we'll be more free to ask questions, seek the truth, and demand accountability from our elected representatives. We'll also be more able to compel our elected representatives to demand accountability from Pentagon officials, the CIA, military officers, and military industries. Asking questions and demanding accountability, after all, require time and effort. Citizen Dividends will ensure that everyone who seeks peace can afford to invest the necessary time.

It will be better for our military, too. Today, many young people enlist because they can't find a job, can't pay their bills, don't have money for college tuition. Economic coercion is bad for morale. When people join the services because they truly want to, our military will be stronger and more effective. We'll be more secure.

Another thing we could do is ask the Iraqi people if they want some version of Citizen Dividends. We could offer to fund it for a few years. The population of Iraq is roughly 25 million, with about 15 million adults. Providing every adult with a basic income of, say, $50 a month would cost just $750 million a month, $9 billion a year. If the basic income is $100 a month, the total would be just $18 billion a year. That's a small fraction of what we are already spending there.

The money would provide every adult Iraqi with some income to rebuild their homes and communities. Every Iraqi – Shiites, Sunnis, Kurds, Turkmen, and others – would have concrete reasons to identify with the whole nation. Every Iraqi would have concrete reasons to seek political reconciliation and stability; reasons to oppose violence and civil war; reasons to support local police and denounce thugs and terrorists. Every Iraqi would have reasons to cooperate with others and seek peace.

Worth a try, don't you think? Why don't we ask the Iraqi people if they like the idea?

People who supported the overthrow of Saddam Hussein might especially welcome this plan. "Iraq's oil belongs to the people of Iraq" — that's what President Bush said before the invasion, and many times since. He promised "to give every Iraqi citizen a stake in the country's economy." Supporters of the war can demonstrate their sincerity and good intentions by endorsing a basic income for Iraqi citizens.

Part of the tragedy of Iraq is that something similar was proposed in 2003, just a few months after the invasion. Senators Lisa Murkowski, a Republican from Alaska, and Mary Landrieu, a Democrat from Louisiana, introduced a resolution to create an "Iraqi Freedom Fund" modeled on the Alaska Permanent Fund Dividend. It would have distributed a portion of Iraq's oil royalties directly to the Iraqi people. The senate held hearings. There were favorable comments from Secretary of State Colin Powell and L. Paul Bremer III, the administrator of U.S. policy in Iraq. Then, however, for reasons that were not reported, the idea was dropped abruptly.*

Something similar could also work in Afghanistan. NATO and European governments are currently providing troops; they might prefer to fund a basic income program. The Afghani people would be in a better position to resolve conflicts between their various factions, and to keep Taliban insurgents from retaking power. Plus, Afghani farmers will have some guaranteed income without planting poppies, so there is likely to be a decline in opium growing and heroin smuggling.

According to many politicians and pundits, stable, democratic governments in Iraq and Afghanistan will lead to progress throughout the region. Our investment in providing them with basic income will pay enormous dividends.

---

* More information about that debate is in Appendix 2.

Can you imagine any faster, better, or cheaper way to achieve stable, democratic governments in Iraq and Afghanistan? Indeed, can you imagine *any* other way to achieve those goals?

We in the United States will save countless many of our soldier's lives.

We'll also save, eventually, hundreds of billions of our taxpayer dollars every year. It is currently almost impossible to cut military spending. Politicians fight passionately to defend the spending in their states and districts, to defend the jobs. Citizen Dividends will change the political dynamics. We individuals and our communities won't be so dependent on military spending and the jobs that spending creates. Political debates about defense, security, and military spending will no longer be distorted by efforts to create jobs. Debates will consequently be more honest. Spending will be more efficient and effective. We'll be more secure.

Is world peace something you think about? Something you dream about or pray for? Is it something you're willing to work to achieve?

There are many ways you can help. A simple and important step is talking to your family members, friends, and neighbors about peace and Citizen Policies; ask them to join you in the campaigns. Write and talk to elected officials. If you work for a company that builds weapons, and you can afford it, you might quit and find another job. You might join pro-peace groups and participate in public protests.

One thing we should all do is demand that our government stop selling or giving weapons to other countries. We also have to demand that our government work with the United Nations and other international agencies to stop weapons sales and transfers by other countries and private companies. We Americans have to take the lead. In the international competition to sell weapons, our government is #1. Approximately 50 percent of all weapons sold around the world are made in the USA.

When our government sells or gives weapons to other countries, it is subsidizing the companies that manufacturer the weapons. To get those subsidies, military companies lobby Congress intensively. They promote themselves and their weapons to the general public. They lobby governments in other countries. They enlist members of Congress and the president to lobby foreign governments on their behalf. That lobbying and marketing brings a huge return on investment. Politicians and lobbyists, when calling for more military spending, typically emphasize the jobs such spending creates — jobs and economic growth. The promise of jobs should not distract us from the facts. Our taxpayer dollars are being used to threaten, endanger, and sometimes kill innocent people in poor countries.

Iraq, Afghanistan, and "terrorism" are not the only wars going on today. There are many places where insurgents are trying to overthrow dictators, ethnic warlords are fighting one another, neighboring countries are disputing a border region. There's fighting in Sudan, Congo, Uganda, Somalia, Chad, Chechnya, Kashmir, Sri Lanka, Columbia, the Philippines, Burma, Nigeria, and elsewhere. And the Middle East.

In each of these places, some things are common: Civilians getting killed. Innocent people starving and suffering. Roads, schools, hospitals, and power plants destroyed. Natural resources despoiled. Pollution and global warming exacerbated. Weapons imported from wealthier countries.

Also common is a large wealth gap. The majority of people in war-afflicted countries are extremely poor, barely getting by, while the ruling elite is very rich. The economic gap is particularly wide in countries that have significant oil or other natural wealth. Noteworthy examples are Congo, Columbia, Sudan, Somalia, Chad, and Nigeria.

Think about a country where fighting is going on. Imagine that a rebel group or political party, or the government, commits to some form of Citizen Dividends. That group or party will quickly gain widespread popular support. Ordinary people will want to resolve conflicts peacefully. Ruling elites might see the benefits of sharing the wealth instead of using it to buy weapons to defend the status quo. The country will soon be on a path toward stability, democracy, and greater prosperity.

If you agree that this seems possible – and if We the People agree, and we demand it – our government could facilitate that progress. We could offer to provide funds and administrative assistance to any country that commits to this path. Our government could ask other wealthy countries and international agencies to join us and provide some of the funding. Versions of this scenario could occur in many countries at the same time. Imagine that. Imagine peace.

Are you concerned about proliferation of nuclear weapons? Officials in our government – and European and U.N. officials – are very concerned, particularly about Iran and North Korea.

When governments seek nuclear weapons, the stated reasons are self-defense, military power, and national prestige. Prestige might appear less important, yet it's very real; when India and Pakistan exploded their first nuclear weapons, ordinary people rallied in the streets to cheer. These reasons, when we examine them more closely, actually refer to the defense, power, and prestige of the ruling political elite or party, or the individual leader — that's who benefits most directly. Ordinary people just pay the bills.

Iran has an elected government, though Islamic clerics have extraordinary authority. A version of Citizen Dividends could help resolve conflicts between the majority of people, who are secular, and the fundamentalist minority. Ordinary Iranians from both communities would surely recognize that it's wasting their money to build or acquire such weapons. It's also hurting them directly, through international economic sanctions and possible military action. Other people and governments have figured that out; Libya, Brazil, Argentina, and South Africa had active programs to build nuclear weapons, and decided to stop.

North Korea's government is a personality cult. The people are desperately poor; they depend on food aid from South Korea, China, Japan, and other countries. Perhaps the providers of that aid can prevail upon Kim Jong Il to present some form of Citizen Dividends as a gift to "his" people. South Korea might offer to pay for the program in the North. That could be the key to reunification, which people in the North and South are reportedly eager to achieve.

These are fantasies, of course, yet quite useful. In politics, as in our personal lives, dreaming about new possibilities is often the first step toward progress. Envisioning a better world is an antidote to feelings of resignation and hopelessness. Resignation and hopelessness – and fear – characterize current attitudes about terrorism, Iraq, Afghanistan, Iran, and North Korea.

What about peace in the Middle East? Could Citizen Policies help resolve conflicts there?

After many decades of ethnic, religious, territorial, and military conflicts, no single reform will bring peace. Yet this would create conditions in which real progress is possible. Think about it.

Ordinary Palestinians have never known economic security, no matter who governed their territory, Turkey, Great Britain, Egypt, Jordan, Israel, or the Palestinian Authority. There have been reports for years that the Palestinian Authority is corrupt, inefficient, ineffectual; that's the main reason for the emergence of Hamas. About half of the 4.1 million Palestinians live below the regional poverty line of $2 a day. Unemployment is more than 40 percent overall, more than 60 percent in some areas.

Suppose the international community offered to provide the funds and help the Palestinians establish their own version of Citizen Dividends. Just $3 billion a year would double the incomes of the poorest. Every Palestinian would have a more direct stake in seeking peace, ending terrorism, and remaking the Palestinian Authority into an effective government that can negotiate with Israel. The plight of the Palestinians will no longer be a rallying point for Hezbollah, Syria, Iran, and other enemies of Israel, including Osama bin Laden and al-Qaeda. Moderate voices might finally be heard over the shouting of militants and fundamentalists.

A few billion dollars a year. That's a lot less than current international aid to the region. It's less, in fact, than the current aid that pays for weapons.

Does this make sense? Could it work, do you think? Have you heard anything else that might lead to peace in the Middle East?

Peace in the Middle East, of course, is not just for the Middle East. War anywhere affects people everywhere. Each of us. All of us. War and preparations for war hasten global climate change. Because of the war in Iraq, we Americans are paying much higher prices for gasoline. Of course, civilians in war-torn countries are affected much more.

At this moment, in wars around the world, children are dying. Children are being killed. Children are being forced to kill. Women and children are being raped. Bombs are destroying food and water supplies, along with schools, hospitals, highways, railroads, power plants, oil refineries, and other infrastructure. Hundreds of millions of people around the world are fighting or preparing for war. The military and related industries provide jobs and incomes, and often a sense of meaning and purpose. Some of the richest, most powerful, and most privileged people and companies are profiting from war and preparations for war; they want to keep their profits and privileges. War is embedded in our everyday behaviors, beliefs, and attitudes. That's the status quo.

That's what we have to challenge and change. We as individuals and we together. We the People.

You can contribute significantly. You can help us achieve peace faster. You could thereby save countless lives.

Is world peace something you think about? Something you dream about or pray for? Are you willing to work for it? Would it help if you didn't have to worry so much about making ends meet?

Part Three
Our Government

We the People of the United States, in order to form a more perfect union, establish justice, insure domestic tranquility, provide for the common defense, promote the general welfare, and secure the blessings of liberty to ourselves and our posterity, do ordain and establish this Constitution for the United States of America.

Preamble, United States Constitution

19

Our Government

Our government is just that, ours. That's what the Declaration of Independence proclaims, and what the Constitution affirms and codifies. We the People are sovereign. We create our government. We own it. We have the right to alter or abolish it.

Are you content with our government? Consider what it's doing or failing to do about crime, health care, education, discrimination, global warming, terrorism. Do you foresee real progress? When?

There are other issues too, of course, including taxes, abortion, gun control, same-sex marriage, embryonic stem-cell research, and campaign finance reform. Regarding these, are you content? Do you foresee real progress?

Think about Citizen Policies. Imagine that every month you are getting an extra $800 and performing some community service. So are your spouse and other adult family members. So are your friends, your neighbors, their neighbors, and every other adult citizen.

What do you suppose that might mean for our government and the way people relate to it? Would you expect people to feel more connected to our government, more dependent on it, more responsible to it and for it? Will people be more likely to demand government that is efficient, accountable, fiscally responsible, and truly democratic? In other words, will people be more likely to act as citizens and participate in improving our government?

What about you, personally? Will you demand more accountability? Will you demand more democracy? Will you act as a citizen?

20

We the People

"We the People" is common political rhetoric. So is "the American people."

Politicians and pundits regularly claim to know what "the people" need, want, think, believe. Ordinary individuals make such statements, too, of course, but our opinions don't count for much. Elected officials have the power to act on their opinions. Pundits have exclusive platforms, opportunities to influence politicians and the rest of us. Plus, politicians and pundits appear to take their opinions seriously, and they expect us to take their opinions seriously.

Both phrases, "We the People" and "the American people," imply some unity, some unanimity. That's partly a function of grammar: "People" refers to multiple individuals as a single unit. Political unity, however, is superficial or transitory — or merely rhetorical. We are divided in many ways, fragmented, sometimes polarized.

This is what makes Citizen Policies so important, so powerful. Every adult citizen will be getting Citizen Dividends. Every adult citizen – almost everyone, anyway – will be performing Citizen Service. Individual citizens will be united more directly than today, united more concretely than today, united more meaningfully than today. Each of us will have constant reminders that we're all in this together.

We the People can make our government more like the one envisioned by Benjamin Franklin, George Washington, John Adams, Thomas Jefferson, James Madison, and their compatriots.

To Form a More Perfect Union

When the Founders wrote the Constitution in 1787, the new nation was in trouble. There were acute conflicts between the states. There were also conflicts between the states and the national government, particularly with regard to raising money. The national government did not have the power to levy taxes, regulate trade, maintain an army, conduct foreign policy, or resolve disputes between the states. "A more perfect union" was not just rhetoric — it was necessary for the nation's survival.

There are conflicts today between states, and between the states and the federal government. Conflicts are evident when politicians talk about "states' rights" and "unfunded mandates." Both phrases are used by critics of labor standards, the minimum wage, No Child Left Behind, and other laws. We see additional conflict when the federal government allocates funds for specific purposes, such as homeland security. Elected officials fight over the money, claiming that their state needs and deserves more, while other states are getting too much.

How should the states relate to each other and to the federal government? What would make the union more perfect, in your opinion?

To answer these questions, it makes sense to start by thinking about individuals. With Citizen Dividends, individual citizens will be getting money from the federal government every month. Each of us will have a more direct relationship with our federal government. Today, the relationship is mostly one-way — we pay taxes. Citizen Dividends will make the relationship more reciprocal, more mutual. Our government will invest in us.

Most of us will spend the money where we live — paying rent, buying food, furnishing our homes, buying clothes, and so on. We'll be stimulating local economic activity and creating local jobs. We'll also be performing Citizen Service, often with church groups, nonprofit agencies, and other organizations that interact with local government. Some of us will serve our local governments more directly, on juries, school boards, neighborhood commissions, community agencies. Our local governments will become more participatory, accountable, and democratic.

At the same time, in the same way, on our own and through our local governments, more of us will be active on statewide issues. We'll be learning about state programs and policies, and communicating with our elected representatives. Our state governments will consequently become more accountable and democratic. Similarly, more of us will be active on national issues, interacting with our federal government. Thus, compared with today, we individuals will have more incentives and opportunities to participate with our government at all levels — and our government will be more responsive to us individuals. The union between us and our government will be more active and interactive, more mutual and reciprocal. More perfect.

The federal government sometimes practices "revenue sharing." That normally means allocating funds to the states on a per capita basis, using federal money to pay for state or local programs. Citizen Dividends is a new type of revenue sharing. It eliminates the middlemen, the state and local bureaucracies, and distributes money directly to every citizen.

Many federal, state, and local government programs will become unnecessary, at least partly. We'll be able to cut or eliminate programs. Cutting government appropriately, making it more efficient and cost-effective, is making it more perfect.

The logic of focusing initially on individuals is in the Constitution. The Ninth Amendment is: "The enumeration in the Constitution of certain rights shall not be construed to deny or disparage others retained by the people." In other words, except for matters explicitly stated in the Constitution, the people retain their rights. Our rights come first. We individuals come first.

The Ninth Amendment is often overlooked. So is the tenth, which complements it and reinforces it. The Tenth Amendment is: "The powers not delegated to the United States by the Constitution, nor prohibited by it to the States, are reserved to the States respectively, or to the people." We come first, before the states. The states come before the federal government. The scope of government is limited. The powers of government are and should be checked, balanced, dispersed.

We can move our nation closer to the Founders' goal. Enacting Citizen Policies will help us form a more perfect union.

Establish Justice

The Constitution is evidence that justice is sometimes sacrificed to political expediency. It initially allowed slavery. It also granted greater political power, in the form of extra representatives, to states that allowed slavery. Without those compromises, southern states would not have ratified it. Slavery in the south, moreover, was lucrative for merchants, manufacturers, and bankers in the north.

Slavery was abolished in 1865, a few months after the end of the Civil War, with the Thirteenth Amendment. Former slaves gained the right to vote in 1870, with the Fifteenth Amendment. Women did not get the right to vote until 1920, with the Nineteenth Amendment.

The Founders sought to establish justice, yet some of them owned slaves. They sought to establish justice, but ignored the rights of women. Those were the values of their time. What about us, today? Are we ignoring injustice? Are current laws and institutions perpetuating injustice? Is our government sacrificing justice to expediency?

Seeking and pursuing justice is a moral duty, according to religious and secular traditions. Central to the American creed, and the concluding phrase in the Pledge of Allegiance, is "liberty and justice for all."

Seeking justice requires us to see injustice. If we don't acknowledge injustice, we cannot correct it. Yet most of us are too busy to look. And many people prefer not to look, prefer to be left alone, not bothered. We typically become aware of injustice only after victims demand our attention. Yet victims of injustice are often relatively voiceless, power-less, marginalized, poor; it's hard for them to get attention and provoke action.

Justice, as the Founders knew, requires laws, courts, juries, and ways to enforce the laws. These institutions are established by government and are part of government. They provide potential redress for victims of injustice. They also protect property, and protecting property is one of government's primary duties. Without laws and police, without government, people could not accumulate wealth.

Justice will be served by enacting Citizen Policies. Every citizen will have some extra income and real economic security. Every citizen, equally. There will be a new baseline of economic equality, more equal access to lawyers and courts, more equal treatment under the law. And greater respect for the law. Each of us will be better protected from being abused, exploited, victimized. Each of us will have greater security in our ability to accumulate property and increase our wealth.

Justice will be served, as well, by more equal opportunities to participate in politics. Active participation is necessary, because politics affects justice in many ways. Elected representatives write laws, select and confirm judges, and determine how laws are enforced. In many states, judges are elected. Attorneys general are elected in almost all states, though not for the federal government. Sheriffs are elected in many towns, cities, and counties.

We individuals have to be active citizens and participate in politics if we sincerely seek to establish justice.

Ensure Domestic Tranquility

The nation was not tranquil when the Founders convened in Philadelphia. An armed uprising in western Massachusetts began in July 1786 and lasted eight months. Shays' Rebellion involved about 4,000 men, most of them veterans and farmers. They had the support of their families and communities, including local officials. They were defending their property, which the state government was threatening to confiscate for taxes.

Shays' Rebellion disturbed the tranquility of people throughout the thirteen states. Most notably, it provoked George Washington to attend the Constitutional Convention; he had refused previous invitations, but he finally agreed to preside. His active participation was vital to the writing and ratification of the Constitution.

Though our nation is generally tranquil today, that could change. Many of us are angry at our government. We're angry about the war in Iraq, immigration, abortion, the cost of health care, the lack of action on global warming. Angry about taxes, too, as were the colonists in 1776 and the rebels in 1786.

Our anger is mixed with fear. What if there's another attack like September 11, or worse? What if there are many small attacks, car bombs in cities around the country?

What if there's another destructive hurricane, like Katrina? Government failed profoundly, local, state, and federal. New Orleans is still vulnerable. So are many other cities. Hurricanes, floods, heat waves, and droughts are forecast to become more common and more severe.

Government officials say they're working to prevent terrorist attacks. They tell us they're preparing for the next natural disaster. Can we trust them? Are they doing their jobs effectively? Their statements could be just public relations for themselves, their party, the current administration.

They may be practicing politics as usual. They may be hiring their friends, putting loyalty before competence, subsidizing special interests, wasting our taxpayer dollars.

Today's tranquility might be superficial. Or delusional. Another terrorist attack or botched response to natural disaster, and our anger and fear could erupt in widespread riots.

As individuals and as a nation, we will be more secure, better prepared, more able to respond effectively to any disturbance, after we have Citizen Policies. Enacting Citizen Policies is a way to ensure domestic tranquility.

Provide for the Common Defense

There was no standing army or navy in 1787. The army was disbanded after winning independence from England; fighting ended in 1781 and a peace treaty was signed in 1783. The nation, however, was vulnerable. States were vulnerable, as Shays' Rebellion showed. Conflicts with Indian tribes appeared inevitable. England was still a military power, the world's leading military power, an empire. Spain and France were also empires, with soldiers and land in North America. Mutual defense made sense, and the Constitution was a pact to provide it.

Today, the United States of America is a superpower. An empire, some people say. Our military spending is roughly equal to the combined military spending of all other nations. The U.S. military has multiple modern weapons systems that are far, far more powerful than the weapons of any other country. The U.S. military maintains more than 730 bases in other countries.

A lot of our military is a remnant of the conflict with the Soviet Union. The Soviet Union collapsed twenty years ago. It could no longer afford to maintain its massive military. It could not compete economically with the United States.

Is our massive military defending us effectively? Is it the best way for us to defend ourselves? Do all of those foreign bases add to our defense and security? Or do some of them actually make us more vulnerable? Are U.S. bases provoking potential terrorists, providing convenient targets for terrorists?

People who ask such questions are often brushed aside. We've seen that done to Republican Ron Paul and Democrat Dennis Kucinich, despite the fact that both have been reelected to Congress many times. We see it also in the way the two major parties and their allied pundits describe – or ignore – Ralph Nader, the Green Party, and the Libertarian Party.

Our defense is compromised, severely, by efforts to create jobs. In debates about defense, security, terrorism, and related issues, it often seems that politicians are most concerned about defending jobs in their states or districts. Defending jobs is politics as usual. Democratic and Republican members of Congress reject closure of military bases the Pentagon says are unneeded, and add more funds than the Pentagon wants for weapons, including the F-22 combat aircraft, the V-22 Osprey, the Virginia class submarine, and missile defense.

Defense and security are too important for that. We have to debate these issues seriously and honestly, without the burden of seeking to create more jobs. Employ as many people as we need, of course, yet no more than we need, no extras. Extra employees deplete resources and drain morale. It's foolish to let political tactics, efforts to create jobs, interfere with defense strategy.

With Citizen Policies, every American citizen will have a secure income independent of any job. That means less political pressure to use military spending to create jobs. We'll be able to have debates about defense that really are about defense.

Our defense and security are compromised also by waste, inefficiency, mismanagement, and lack of accountability in the Pentagon. Investigations by Democrats, Republicans, and independent auditors have documented myriad serious errors and abuses. Tens of billions of dollars are wasted every year. We have to demand more accountability from our elected representatives. They have to demand more accountability from the military and military industries. We and they have to demand, in particular, far more accountability on privatization of military functions. Citizen Policies will empower us to make those demands.

Defense includes deterrence. Deterrence can be economic as well as military. When We the People are more united, less divided by competition and class resentment, we'll be able to use our economic power more effectively. Our economic power is much greater than our military power. There are many ways to use it. By reducing our oil consumption, we might deter military activity by Iran, Russia, and other oil-exporting countries. By importing less stuff and renegotiating trade agreements, we might deter China from expanding its military. Economic power, releasing funds that had been withheld, prompted North Korea to shut down its nuclear reactor in July, 2007. Economic power, aid and trade, is vital for progress toward peace among the Palestinians, between the Palestinians and Israel, and throughout the Middle East. Defense and the military are subject to civilian control, and that's a founding principle under our Constitution. We the People have to be actively involved. We ordinary individuals, in particular, have to be active regarding terrorism. We have to be vigilant. Terrorist attacks in the United States and on Americans abroad are likely, almost certain.

Terrorism is a tactic. It's the weapon weak people use to attack a superpower. The U.S. military has cruise missiles, stealth bombers, aircraft carriers, spy satellites, and nuclear weapons. Terrorists have car bombs and improvised explosive devices. The attackers on September 11 used box cutters, ten-cent razor blades.

Terror is a state of mind. People in Iraq and Afghanistan have been terrorized and traumatized. Hundreds of thousands of civilians have been killed or wounded. Many women. Many children. The killed and wounded have hundreds of millions of friends, relatives, sympathizers, and supporters around the world. Some of those people, possibly many, may seek revenge by attacking Americans.

War is terrible. War is terrifying. War, even a "war on terror" or "war on terrorism," produces terror and terrorists.

To reduce terrorism and eventually end it, we have to reduce terror — everywhere, for everyone. We have to reassure people in Iraq, Iran, Afghanistan, North Korea, Pakistan, and other countries, all other countries, that we truly seek peace. Citizen Policies will help us do that. We can close some foreign bases, perhaps a lot of them. We can eliminate wasteful military spending, and start to make prudent cuts. We might use some of the money we save to provide aid and promote trade with hostile countries, engaging and encouraging them to become partners. We might help other countries establish their own versions of Citizen Dividends.

An argument for maintaining our massive military, a fairly common argument, is that we need it to preserve our access to foreign oil. Is our military really necessary for that? How? Why? China, Japan, India, Germany, and other countries just buy their oil. We buy our oil, too. We'll still be able to buy it if we cut our military. We'll be more able to afford it. Plus, cutting our military will slow global warming. The U.S. military is the world's biggest consumer of fossil fuels and the world's biggest producer of greenhouse gases.

We'll be much safer with Citizen Policies. We'll be much better able to provide for the common defense.

Promote the General Welfare

In the Constitution, Article 1, Section 8 begins, "The Congress shall have power to lay and collect taxes, duties, imposts and excises, to pay the debts and provide for the common defense and general welfare of the United States." General welfare, right up there with national defense and national obligations or debts. *General* welfare refers to all people, as distinct from the *special* welfare of certain people or corporations.

Citizen Policies will promote the general welfare directly, efficiently. Every adult citizen will have some income, enough to guarantee basic welfare. Every adult citizen will also have greater means and incentives to pursue the common good, the public interest. Common good. Public interest. General welfare.

In contrast, most government policies promote *special welfare* — special welfare of specific people, groups, businesses, industries, regions of the country. There are subsidies and tax credits, pork-barrel spending and congressional earmarks. Some of those measures are publicly debated. Others are hidden. Elected officials use various tactics to conceal their efforts to help special interests; that's normal, politics as usual. Hidden costs include the economic and public health costs associated with our addiction to oil. In most industrialized countries, the social costs of oil consumption are reflected in the price at the pump, which is typically more than twice what we pay in the United States. Here, oil prices are kept deceptively low by socializing part of the true cost.

Policies that promote the special welfare – any special welfare, regardless of the specifics – are usually defended as ways to create jobs. Haven't you read or heard that, "creating jobs," countless times? Isn't that the stated reason for most subsidies, tax credits, and earmarks?

Creating jobs is presumed to be a legitimate task for government, even a fundamental duty. But there's nothing in the Constitution about creating jobs. The word "jobs" is not used, not even once. There's also nothing about "the economy" or "economic growth." The Founders did not envision any direct government role in creating jobs and promoting economic growth.

Special welfare is actually *bad* for the general welfare, bad for our nation. Policies that provide any sort of special welfare are divisive, inherently and unavoidably divisive. Programs to create jobs are good for the people who get the jobs, and good for elected officials, who can boast about creating jobs when they campaign for reelection. The rest of us pay the bills through higher taxes. We are divided: the special few who benefit from a program vs. the majority who pay for it.

Special welfare distorts markets. The jobs, goods, services, and activities that get the subsidies are favored. Other jobs, goods, services, and activities become relatively more expensive. Subsidies to create jobs, for example, cause employers in other businesses or industries to pay higher labor costs or hire less qualified workers.

Special welfare constrains or biases our choices as consumers. Subsidies and tax credits go to big companies and industries that can afford to hire lobbyists. Almost nothing goes to small and independent businesses. Wal-Mart and Home Depot get subsidies; neighborhood grocers and hardware stores do not. Farm subsidies are another example. Our government gives billions of dollars a year to big agribusiness corporations that produce corn syrup, soybeans, and wheat. Those are main ingredients in processed foods, which are quite cheap because of the subsidies. Organic farmers who grow fruits and vegetables are mostly on their own, without financial support. Many Americans are obese, unhealthy; one reason is the way our government subsidizes junk food.

Politicians often say they're eager to reform government. They want to eliminate earmarks and pork-barrel spending, they say, and simplify the tax code to get rid of tax breaks and subsidies. But they seem to be unable to do that. The primary goal of elected officials, after all, is to get reelected. They know they're more likely to be reelected when they promote the special welfare of wealthy constituents and campaign contributors.

The general welfare will be guaranteed with Citizen Policies, or at least the basics — food and shelter. Special welfare will normally be unnecessary, and hard to justify. It will therefore be easier for us to eliminate programs that benefit special interests. We individuals, We the People, and our government can then work together in other ways to promote the general welfare.

And Secure the Blessings of Liberty

The world of the Founders was very different from our world today. Americans were farmers, and farms were small. Other people owned small, independent businesses, or worked for small businesses. People grew food, made their own clothes, built homes and furniture, bought and sold stuff among their friends and neighbors. Imported goods were expensive. Towns and communities were self-governing, primarily, and most people participated in local government through town meetings. Newspapers were local too, written, edited, and published by people who lived in the community.

Now, most of us work for big, faceless corporations. Our food comes from supermarkets; it's grown, produced, manufactured somewhere far away — we're not sure where. Our clothes and household goods are made in China. Many of us don't know our neighbors. Few of us participate in politics. Half of us rarely vote, if ever. News and entertainment are provided by global media corporations.

Are these the "blessings of liberty" the Founders had in mind?

What does liberty mean to you, personally? How do you experience the blessings of liberty? When do you feel free, independent?

Compared with people in 1787 – or 1887, or even 1987 – we are much more dependent. We depend on big corporations for income, food, shelter, and health care; in other words, we depend on them for our survival. We depend on big corporations for transportation, communication, and entertainment. Increasingly, we depend on corporations to deploy our armed forces and fight our wars, and to incarcerate prisoners of our criminal justice system. In some places, we depend on corporations to teach our children and run our schools. We depend on government to stop corporations from poisoning us, exploiting us, ripping us off.

"Liberty" is on our coins. An aspect of liberty is having money. Enjoying liberty often involves spending money. Many of us, however, are not so free. We're burdened by credit card debt, living from paycheck to paycheck, afraid of losing our jobs, worried about how to pay our bills. Are financial pressures curtailing your liberty? Would you feel more free if we had Citizen Policies?

Suppose you and your spouse are each getting $800 a month, independent of your jobs. So are your parents and your adult children. Think about that, and how it would affect your liberty, your freedom, your independence.

One idea of liberty, a common idea, is being self-employed. Making the decisions. Being your own boss. Is that something you dream about? Is there a type of business you'd like to own? Starting a business will be a lot easier, and less risky.

Freedom can mean being able to devote more time to our families. Would you like to be a full-time parent? Or to work part-time while you care for your elderly parents? Those choices will be more financially feasible.

A feeling of freedom can come with a truly satisfying job or career. Some careers offer real satisfaction and other rewards, but low pay. Nursing and teaching in elementary schools are examples. Citizen Dividends would supplement the pay, facilitating the choice of those careers. That applies also to creative pursuits such as writing, acting, making videos, and playing music.

Independence is often associated with retirement. Freedom to travel, for hobbies, to learn and do things that have been deferred. Extra retirement income would make a huge difference for tens of millions of us.

Every citizen will be more free to pursue his or her dreams. Every citizen will be more able to enjoy the blessings of liberty.

To Ourselves and Our Posterity

Americans in 1787 were mutually interdependent. They needed each other. And they knew it. Families and neighbors worked together, and had to work together on farming, building homes, and other regular activities. Communities worked together to build and maintain roads, bridges, churches, schools.

We still need each other. Many of us, however, don't know it or won't admit it. Many of us think it makes sense to just mind our own business. Many of us think we'll be okay, no matter what happens to our neighbors, if we just earn enough money.

Earn enough money, people believe, and anyone can have the American dream. A big house, perhaps in a gated community with security guards. Private schools. A nice car, so there's no need for public transportation. With enough money, life is good.

Do you have a big house and nice car? Are you happy? No matter how big the house or nice the car, the world intrudes. Nothing can change that, not even a private jet and several houses. (Very big houses and private jets, in fact, come with added intrusions. Such possessions require pilots, personal assistants, security guards, household staff. Each employee has unique needs, and the potential to cause problems.) The world intrudes, and there's no way to keep it out. Disease. Pollution. Global warming. Economic instability. Social unrest. War. Terrorism.

For ourselves and our posterity, we have to recover the sense that we're all in this together. Americans knew that not too long ago, within the lifetimes of many us. During World War II, people bought war bonds, planted victory gardens, collected rubber and scrap metal, conserved gasoline. People around the country were eager and happy to contribute, participate, volunteer, serve. "We're all in this together" was not just something people said. They lived it. A lot of us felt that way for a few days immediately after September 11.

A simple yet significant step in that direction is Citizen Service. Every adult citizen will be serving in some way, contributing in some way, each in accordance with his or her particular concerns. Working for the general welfare. Pursuing the common interest.

Citizen Service will transform our values and ideas about what it means to be a citizen. Service will be customary.

Though some people might shirk, social pressure will make that rather rare, particularly over time as the new norms become stronger. Changing the norms and expectations may be even more valuable than the service itself. We individuals will more truly be We the People, more like Americans during World War II. Or on September 12. Possibly more like Americans in 1787.

The Founders sought to secure the blessings of liberty for all Americans for generations to come. Our posterity. Today, it's rare for people to think so grandly and inclusively. We are typically concerned about our own posterity only, our children and grandchildren.

What will the United States of America be in 50 or 100 years? Do you think the nation will still be a democracy? Will the Constitution still be in effect? Could the government become a dictatorship with sham elections?

The world will be very different. In 50 or 100 years, if scientists are right about global warming, even imprecisely right, vast coastal areas will be underwater. Tens of millions of people will have lost their homes, jobs, incomes. The losses will not be gradual and predictable, but in sudden bursts like Hurricane Katrina. Inland cities will be terribly overcrowded. Water will cover toxic waste dumps and nuclear reactors, perhaps killing fish and crops. Food and clean water might be scarce. Rioting and social unrest might be commonplace.

That could be the world of our posterity. If we stay on the present course.

We can change direction. Citizen Policies is a way to reawaken the vision of the Founders, and to help fulfill that vision. The sooner we act, the better it will be for ourselves and our posterity.

21

Economics

Economic issues and policies are confusing, for lots of reasons. Economists disagree about the data. They dispute theories and debate interpretations. They use specialized jargon and mathematical symbols. Their statements are often vague, ambivalent, or nearly incomprehensible — and that may be intentional, particularly when they're speaking on the record about public policies.

Politicians take only the data, theories, and interpretations that validate their biases. When talking about economic issues, they repeat and reaffirm their campaign slogans. They rarely say anything more substantial. They almost never express doubts.

Perhaps the politicians don't understand economics. Has that ever occurred to you? What if elected officials don't know what they're talking about?

Sometimes economists agree with one another and communicate clearly. In the 1960s, Milton Friedman and John Kenneth Galbraith, separately, called for guaranteed income. They were two of America's leading economists, authors of bestselling books, identified respectively with the far right and far left of their profession. Several of their colleagues circulated a letter in 1968 that called on Congress "to adopt this year a national system of income guarantees and supplements." More than 1,200 economists signed the letter, including many who worked for government. Prominent signers included Galbraith; Paul Samuelson, who was awarded the Nobel Memorial Prize in Economics in 1970; and James Tobin, who received the Nobel prize in 1981.

Citizen Policies will reconnect economic policies with our everyday realities. We ordinary citizens will be more able to understand the issues. That means we'll be more able to participate actively in making policies. We won't be so dependent on economists, pundits, politicians, and self-proclaimed "experts."

Economic policies will more truly serve our needs and interests.

"The Economy" is a Fiction

The economy, we're often told, is strong, healthy, growing. Sometimes we're told it's slowing down, of course. There are endless debates about the details, disputes about the rate of growth and other statistics. Despite the uncertainties, the dominant message is consistent and optimistic.

Do you sometimes wonder: "If the economy is strong, why am I struggling to pay my bills?" "Why am I at risk of losing my job?" "Why can't I get ahead?" "Am I doing something wrong?"

Maybe it's not your fault. A majority of us *are* struggling. Over the past three decades, particularly the past eight years, most of the benefits of economic growth have gone to the

wealthiest 20 percent of the population, especially to the top
1 percent, overwhelmingly to the top 0.1 percent. As for the
rest of us, many are in worse shape financially than we were
10 or 20 or 30 years ago. Income inequality – the gap between
the very rich and the rest of us – is greater now than at any
time since the 1920s. These facts have been thoroughly documented and widely reported. The facts, however, are mostly
drowned out and disregarded.

For each person who discusses income inequality or
economic insecurity, there are dozens who say the economy
is healthy. The economy's strengths are touted by bankers,
stockbrokers, CEOs, realtors, and developers, in addition
to politicians, pundits, and economists. Elected officials do
more — when they tell us how strong the economy is, they
claim credit. And they tell us we need to reelect them to keep
it strong and growing.

The economy created 50,000 jobs last month.

*The economy grew at a 2 percent rate in the last
quarter.*

*The economy is strong, even with the decline in housing
prices.*

*The economy's fundamentals are sound and the stock
market will rebound.*

We hear such statements just about every day. Have
you ever thought about what they really mean? What is "the
economy"?

There is no formal definition for "the economy" — not
even among economists. To call it "healthy" or "growing"
suggests that it's a living being. It's not, obviously. To say it
creates jobs is also false. People create jobs for themselves

and others, and companies create jobs when they hire more workers. "The economy" is not a person or a company. It has never created a single job.

Most often, "the economy" is a summary term for the money-related aspects of our society. It represents a blend of statistics and general perceptions. Normally highlighted are statistics about unemployment, inflation, interest rates, and gross domestic product. Secondary indicators are the stock market, housing construction, sale of existing homes, and consumer confidence.

"The economy" can also refer specifically to gross domestic product; some people use these terms as synonyms. The GDP is the total of every economic transaction in the United States, the dollar value of everything produced or sold, all the goods and services. Just add it all up, and that's the GDP.

When someone buys a new car, the GDP goes up. It goes up more if there's an accident, the car is totaled, and the person buys another car. It goes up even more, much more, if the accident is serious, people are hurt, and there are lawsuits. Serious accidents create jobs and income for police officers, medics, doctors, nurses, tow-truck drivers, insurance agents, and lawyers. The GDP goes up when our government buys tanks, trucks, Humvees, helicopters, and other military equipment. It goes up more and faster when the equipment is blown up and has to be replaced.

The GDP is truly gross. It disregards how money is earned or spent, whether wisely or wastefully, productively or destructively. It counts war, crime, disease, pollution, and wasted government spending as positive line-items. The more war, crime, disease, pollution, and wasted government spending, the faster the GDP goes up. Measuring "the economy" in terms of the GDP, in other words, gives elected officials incentives to start wars and waste our taxpayer dollars. Elected officials spend our money, even waste our money; the GDP goes up; then the officials claim credit for creating economic growth.

There are alternatives to the GDP. Economists can total up the spending and economic activities that enhance our lives, and subtract that which detracts. Count and add the good stuff; discount and subtract the bad. The idea is to measure overall quality of life. That's complicated, obviously. It requires assigning some dollar value to the harms that come with layoffs, traffic jams, computer viruses, and economic insecurity. Even so, a number of economists have devised ways to do it. According to the alternative indicators, quality of life has been declining for several decades, since the mid-1970s.

"The economy" must be society's servant, not its master; must work to create better living conditions for workers, not just higher profits for investors; must be not an end in itself but a means to enhancing quality of life consistent with our real needs and values.

With Citizen Policies, every citizen will have a decent quality of life, guaranteed. And economic data will indicate that.

Unemployment

The unemployment rate is often in the news. When it's too high, people want government to act and create jobs. When it's too low, people become concerned about inflation and rising prices. Just right, supposedly, is around 4.5 percent. Economists call that the "natural rate of unemployment."

The natural rate accounts for "churning" — workers quitting jobs and looking for new ones, companies dissolving and new companies forming.

The unemployment rate only counts people who are actively looking for full-time jobs. That's the official definition of "unemployment." Thus, many people are not working and not counted as unemployed.

Not counted, most notably, are those who have given up looking. That's a lot of people, particularly in rural areas and inner-city neighborhoods. Some inner cities have an official unemployment rate of 10 to 20 percent for young black and Latino men; by most estimates the actual rate is two to three times higher. Also not actively looking, and therefore not counted, are millions of people who are too busy or too tired to look. There are people working two or three part-time jobs. There are many individuals with real skills – engineers, carpenters, machinists, and so on – who are driving taxis or greeting customers at Wal-Mart.

Some people are not counted as either employed or unemployed — full-time parents, for example, and caregivers for family members who are elderly or disabled. Caregiving is real work, necessary and valuable work, but mostly not compensated and consequently not counted. As individuals and as a society, however, we rely on caregivers far more than on, say, pundits.

Unemployment causes or correlates with poverty, hunger, homelessness, crime, and disease. Current efforts to solve these problems depend on creating jobs, preparing people for jobs, getting people to take jobs and stay in them — and our government spends a lot of our money for those purposes. Yet there will always be people who do not work or cannot work.

With Citizen Policies, every adult citizen will have income for food and shelter, guaranteed, whether employed or unemployed. Fear of unemployment will no longer be a dominant force in public policy decisions. As a society, we won't have to be so concerned about unemployment.

As individuals, each of us will be more free. Fear of unemployment will not be so coercive in our personal decisions. Each of us will be more free to seek work that is meaningful, dignified, and satisfying.

What's meaningful for you? Are you happy in your current job, career, profession? Would you be more satisfied doing something else? Think about it. Consider what you want to do for the rest of your life, or perhaps just the next year or two.

Are you looking to get rich? Is a specific career important to you? Would you like to start your own business, to be self-employed? Might you enjoy teaching or nursing, even though it doesn't pay very much? Is your goal to earn enough so your spouse can be a full-time caregiver, or to have your spouse work and earn enough so you can stay home? Are you primarily looking for a steady paycheck, so you can devote your attention to family, friends, hobbies, artistic pursuits, community service, faith and religious activities?

Such questions can be a luxury or a distraction. Many of us have credit card debt, college loans, no health insurance, not enough money saved for retirement. Many of us have to take whatever jobs we can find. That can mean unsatisfying, dead-end jobs. Or jobs that might be okay, but the pay is too low or the boss is a jerk. An unsatisfying job is a real barrier to the pursuit of happiness.

It will be a lot easier to find or create satisfying work when we have Citizen Policies. And our government – local, state, and national – will be relieved of any presumed responsibility to provide jobs. The money that currently goes to those efforts will be available to help fund Citizen Dividends.

Inflation

Inflation – rising prices for food, housing, gasoline, and other goods and services – can cause real problems, particularly for people with low or fixed incomes. Problems for businesses, too. When their costs go up, businesses sometimes have to increase the prices they charge their customers; that can mean losing customers. Employers sometimes have to downsize and fire workers. That's how inflation can lead to higher unemployment.

With Citizen Policies, we won't have to be so concerned about inflation. Government will have a new tool to prevent harms and hardships. When necessary, whenever inflation is high, we can increase the amount of Citizen Dividends. Those increases won't cause further inflation if they're coordinated with government actions on taxes and spending. Increases might also be coordinated with inflation-fighting efforts by the Federal Reserve Board. Citizen Dividend adjustments might be automatic according to some formula based on cost of living.

Economic conditions will be more stable and predictable. That will be good for individuals, families, businesses, and government. Greater economic stability and predictability are especially desirable as we confront globalization, climate change, technological change, and declining fossil fuel supplies. Current economic models portray inflation and unemployment as a seesaw — when one goes up, the other goes down. That situation will stabilize with Citizen Policies. Neither inflation nor unemployment will be the serious concerns they are today.

Recession

Economic downturns or recessions are inevitable, according to most economists. Also inevitable, therefore, are loss of jobs, lower wages, and other economic difficulties that occur with recessions.

Our government currently has three strategies for ending recessions or trying to prevent them: cutting taxes, lowering interest rates, and increasing government spending. Each approach works by putting more money into circulation. With each, however, the results are delayed, indirect, unreliable, and unevenly distributed. That's why it can take years for our society to recover from a recession. That's also why some individuals, families, and businesses never recover.

When we have Citizen Dividends, we can simply increase the amount. That will put more money into circulation promptly, directly, reliably, and universally. Every individual will be protected from hardships. Businesses and communities will also be protected.

Interest Rates

Interest rates are set by the Federal Reserve Board. The Fed has considerable power to affect economic conditions, including inflation, unemployment, and our ability to prevent or recover from recessions. Its actions affect us individuals as well — the amount we pay for mortgages, student loans, and credit card debt. The Fed is composed of bankers and economists. Members are appointed by the President and Congress. We the People have only indirect influence over who's on it and what it does.

The Fed controls the money supply. Literally. It loans money to other banks and the federal government. It lowers the interest rate it charges when it wants to stimulate faster economic growth. It raises interest rates when it wants to reduce or prevent inflation. Lower rates promote borrowing, investment, housing construction, and related activities; high rates have the opposite effect, depressing those economic activities.

Citizen Dividends will give our government added tools to reduce inflation, promote economic stability, and speed recovery from recessions. The Fed will consequently be less powerful. Changes in interest rates will have less impact.

Taxes

How should government assess and collect taxes? What would be best? Most fair? Most efficient? Least intrusive?

The income tax system is a mess, and everyone knows it. The tax code has tens of thousands of pages, written in dense, bureaucratic legal jargon that's incomprehensible to most of us. Billions of hours a year are required for people to fill out tax forms, keep records, try to interpret the rules and regulations, and comply with intimidating audits. That time and effort – and the associated costs to individuals, families, businesses, and government – are a huge drain on our productivity. Also a huge drain on our happiness.

Politicians talk about tax cuts and tax reform. The "reforms" they propose, however, almost always make taxes more complicated. Democrats and Republicans use the tax code to provide special interests with tax breaks. That's business as usual, politics as usual. Politicians promise tax cuts and tax credits. Special interests respond with campaign contributions.

Tax breaks and credits promote the special welfare, not the general welfare. Often, in fact, tax credits are "targeted," designed to promote some specific political purpose. Examples include first-time home buyers, parents of college students, and specific industries or communities. The ends may be worthy public policy, but the means are divisive.

Tax credits are coercive. It's social engineering, rewarding people who act in specific ways. In many cases, moreover, people who are targeted and supposed to benefit don't get the credits. Tax credits to promote savings, for example, mostly benefit members of the upper middle class, not the poor, because the poor don't earn enough money to save. With tax credits to get people to buy health insurance, insurance companies are major beneficiaries.

A lot of people, including some politicians, say we should just get rid of the current tax system. Replace it with something simpler, more sensible and efficient, more just and equitable.

One fundamental reform with widespread support is a flat income tax. "File your return on a postcard," proponents claim. Opponents say a flat tax would harm the poor, who have to spend a higher percentage of their income on necessities. True; but when we have tax-free Citizen Dividends, a flat income tax with no deductions would work beautifully. Just about everyone would benefit.

Suppose we have Citizen Dividends of $10,000 a year and a flat tax rate of 20 percent. If you have no income, perhaps because you're a full-time parent, you'll get the $10,000 and pay nothing. If you earn $50,000 a year, the 20 percent flat tax will be $10,000, equal to your Citizen Dividends; the net will be $0, the net rate 0 percent. If you earn $100,000, taxes will be $20,000, minus $10,000 for Citizen Dividends; the net will be a $10,000 tax liability, equal to a 10 percent rate. If you earn $200,000, the net will be a $30,000 liability, 15 percent. And so on. As income increases, the net approaches the full 20 percent rate. Flat. Fair. Easy to understand. Simple to calculate. Simple to administer.

What do you think? Do you like the idea of a flat tax combined with Citizen Dividends?

Another popular proposal is a national sales tax. "Abolish the IRS," say proponents, who call this "the Fair Tax." It would eliminate the income tax along with payroll taxes, estate taxes, gift taxes, capital gains taxes, and corporate taxes. Proponents calculate that a 23 percent tax on retail purchases would provide the same revenue as the current system. To protect the poor, to offset taxes on food and other necessities, there would be a "prebate." At the start of each month, every household would receive a cash payment. It would be $196 for a single person, $391 for a couple, $525 for a couple with two children, and more than that for larger households. Citizen Dividends can serve the same purpose as the proposed prebate, and much more simply.

A national sales tax would make tax payments obvious to everyone; the system would be transparent, nothing hidden.

Paychecks would include 100 percent of pay, minus only state income taxes. Corporations would no longer have to set prices to cover their taxes, so prices would fall. Compared to the current system, there would be greater incentives to save, invest, pursue education, start businesses, create jobs. Government would be smaller, less intrusive, more efficient and cost-effective. Almost every state has a sales tax already, so a national sales tax would be relatively simple to implement and administer.

Would you rather pay taxes when you make purchases, instead of April 15th? Does a national retail sales tax make sense to you?

A third model for fundamental reform is to tax consumption of natural resources. "Tax what people take, not what we make." Taxes would be on whatever people take from nature. That includes oil, coal, timber, minerals, water, and land, plus the use of electromagnetic spectrum for telecommunications. The tax would be a fee or "rent" for the right to use, consume, or pollute natural resources. Collecting the tax at the point of the taking, instead of at the gas pump or cash register, is a way to promote market-driven efficiencies in every economic activity. It would reduce waste and reward recycling.

Proponents say oil, coal, and other resources are provided by nature or God, and are therefore our common property, our commonwealth. Profits from privatizing the commonwealth ought to be shared. An early advocate was Thomas Paine, who described land as the "common heritage of mankind." He called for owners of land to pay a "ground rent," with everyone receiving a share through a cash payment at age 21 and yearly payments starting at age 50. Modern advocates apply the concept to all natural resources. That's the logical basis for the Alaska Permanent Fund Dividend. Most resources are already assessed and taxed, though only lightly, so implementing this reform would be quite simple.

Are resource consumption taxes a good idea, do you think? Would you like to see this type of tax shift?

There are other reform proposals, of course, many others. There are also many ways to combine these three major reforms and others. With politics as usual, however, real tax reform will never happen. It can't. The current system is too lucrative for too many special interests that fight to protect their profits and privileges. We're stuck with the current income tax – probably made even more complicated, intrusive, oppressive – until We the People demand better.

Advocates of tax reform can succeed by deferring debates about specific plans, and first calling for Citizen Policies. Would you like $800 a month, tax free? Might that prospect motivate you to join your friends, neighbors, and other people, and work together for progress on taxes and other economic issues?

Ordinary Americans will be more engaged as citizens. The special interests will have less influence. We'll be able to have good, productive debates about what taxes would be best, most fair, most efficient, and least intrusive. We'll be able to get serious about reform.

Deficits and the Federal Debt

Deficits don't matter, some people say. Trade deficits, budget deficits, and the long-term federal debt are not important. Economic growth will take care of the problems. Markets will adjust.

Other people describe deficits and debt as monsters lurking just out of sight, waiting to devour us. Those monsters include Medicare, Medicaid, and Social Security. These three big entitlement programs operate through trust funds, which are supposed to be set aside for that purpose. But the trust funds are running out of money. Baby Boomers are starting to retire, increasing the demand for funds, making the situation more and more precarious. Medicare is most at risk, though Social Security gets far more attention.

What are elected officials doing about these issues? Not much. They seem to be afraid to call for any specific action. The extent of their political courage, it appears, is to propose a bipartisan commission to study the situation and present recommendations.

It will be much easier for us to make good choices after we enact Citizen Policies. Real tax reform will help enormously. With a flat income tax or national sales tax, it will be relatively simple to adjust tax rates when necessary to balance budgets or reduce deficits. We'll also be able to adjust the amount of Citizen Dividends. Either type of adjustment will affect everyone. There will be no basis for special interests to mobilize in opposition. We'll be much more able to act responsibly on Medicare and Social Security. It will even be possible to pay off the federal debt for the first time since 1835.

Productivity and Economic Growth

Citizen Policies will boost productivity, especially if they open the political door to serious tax reform. Economic growth will be more rapid than it is today, and it will benefit ordinary

Americans more directly. Economic growth, moreover, will no longer be defined by unemployment, inflation, interest rates, or the GDP. The conventional indicators may still be useful, but they will be less relevant. Instead, economic growth will be measured by quality of life indicators such as health, literacy, educational attainment, leisure time, and life expectancy. Improving quality of life will be the goal of public policy. We won't have to be so concerned about "the economy."

To see how and why we can expect these gains, think about productivity in personal terms. When are you most productive? When are you most creative? When do you work harder and accomplish the most?

The answers, for most of us, are obvious. We're more productive and creative, and we work harder, when doing work that is meaningful and satisfying. Right? Isn't that true for you? Isn't the opposite also true, that you're less productive and less motivated when you feel dissatisfied or coerced?

With Citizen Policies, each of us, all of us, will be more free to choose meaningful, satisfying work. Free to choose among existing jobs and other opportunities. Free to create our own opportunities.

Many of us – more than today, certainly – will start businesses. That's something a lot of people dream about. Many of us, however, are deterred by the financial risks. It will be less risky when every citizen has a guaranteed basic income. Entrepreneurs will be more secure, will know that they can at least afford food and shelter throughout the months or years it takes to launch a business.

Small businesses have been the main engine of productivity and economic growth throughout American history. Small businesses create many more jobs than big corporations. Small businesses, moreover, sometimes grow into big businesses. One or two people with an idea started Apple, Google, Wal-Mart, Ford, McDonalds, and every other big company.

Productivity will also grow and economic growth will also speed up because working people will have more money to spend. People will demand goods and services. Those demands will drive growth and stimulate businesses to produce.

Plus, more of us will save and invest. At least we'll have money that we can save and invest. Current efforts to promote savings rely mostly on tax cuts, tax credits, and tax deductions. Such tax policies do little to help working people. You can't invest a tax credit in a 401(k) plan. Would you be more likely to save money for retirement if your basic needs were met by Citizen Dividends?

Productivity and economic growth will also gain, in most cases, when people quit unsatisfying jobs. Those jobs will become available. Jobs will be taken by workers who are more satisfied. Employers know that satisfied workers are more productive. Employers will benefit, as well, by being more able to hire people part-time or to contract the work instead of hiring. Thus, employers will gain greater flexibility. That means greater profitability, particularly for small and start-up businesses.

People who quit their jobs won't have any claim on extra government funds or services. Those who are not actively looking for other jobs won't even be counted as unemployed.

It will be good for productivity and economic growth – and good for society generally – when each of us has the freedom to say "no" to a regular full-time job. Most of us will work full-time anyway, to maximize earnings and savings. Some of us will work part-time, or on our own, flexible schedules. Freedom to choose, after all, includes the freedom to be unemployed or underemployed. Besides, when people can afford to quit, they might more readily find meaning and satisfaction in their current jobs. The freedom to say "no" enhances the freedom to sincerely say "yes."

Parents might choose to be full-time parents, to devote themselves to raising healthy children, and that will be very good for our society. Some of us will work part-time while dedicating ourselves to art, music, writing, science, or other creative pursuits, perhaps eventually doing, creating, or discovering something valuable. Creativity takes time, after all; it's a subtle and somewhat unpredictable process. Even people who appear to be doing nothing might make real contributions. The Wright Brothers, Philo Farnsworth, and Benjamin Franklin were dilettantes and hobbyists when they made their most important advances in technology.

We can expect greater productivity and economic growth, in addition, from other aspects of Citizen Policies. Crime is a huge drain on productivity. So are pollution, poor health, and war. So are bad government, wasteful spending, and the current tax system. Citizen Policies will facilitate progress in each of these areas.

Economic issues will be more comprehensible; we ordinary citizens will be able to understand the issues. We'll be less dependent on economists and politicians, and we'll have more practical freedom to participate actively in making policies. Economic policies will truly serve our needs and interests.

22

Politics

Politics today, politics as usual, often seems like a game or sport. Democrats vs. Republicans. Conservatives vs. liberals. Opposing teams, competing intensely, competing continuously. Within the teams, too, people compete for leading positions. Journalists cover the competition in detail, with frequent stories about strategies and tactics, polls and momentum. Fundraising is reported like box scores. Pundits act like cheerleaders or coaches second-guessing from the sidelines. Journalists and pundits appear to enjoy the competition, and that makes sense. Sports, after all, are entertaining. Sports are exciting. Sports are fun. Journalists and pundits are in the middle of the action.

In politics, as in other competitions, the focus is on winning. Winning elections. Winning debates. Winning the votes on specific issues. Or, whenever a vote goes the other way, claiming a moral or tactical victory, claiming to have gained public support, claiming to be better prepared for the next round.

Appearances matter. Acting like a winner, appearing "electable," is good. Politicians who act like winners – confident, optimistic, resolute, authentic, cheerful, likeable, fun to be around – typically get more positive media attention. They attract contributors, volunteers, and voters. They also attract endorsements from other politicians, who are seeking to enhance their own status and prospects by endorsing the likely winner. We Americans like winners. We like winning. We want to be #1. We feel good, proud, smart, happy, when our team or candidate wins.

But winning is not governing. The drive and desire to win can make it harder to govern.

Governing normally involves seeking unity, and frequently means compromising. Governing successfully requires real leadership. Real leaders have the courage to seek compromises that are in the public interest, even compromises that demand some sacrifice. Real leaders have the skill to gain support for compromises. Real leaders are honest and thoughtful enough to change their positions when necessary, and to explain the change openly. Sometimes, of course, real leaders must have the courage to stand on principle and refuse to compromise. Those occasions are rare. The day-to-day business of governing is relatively tedious, detailed, hard work — seeking consensus, negotiating compromises.

Competition is much more exciting. That's one reason our political system is so paralyzed, polarized, stalemated. Democrats vs. Republicans, conservatives vs. liberals.

Our political system is broken and everyone knows it. Fundamental change is necessary, and most of us want it.

We ordinary Americans, by the millions, are abandoning the Democratic and Republican parties. About 40 percent of us now identify as independents. Many of us are joining the Green Party, Libertarian Party, or some other "third" party.

A lot of us are giving up, turning off, refusing to participate. That's not surprising, though it's self-defeating, even self-destructive. It cedes power to the special interests. Special interests profit from exploiting our government; they're highly motivated. When we ordinary citizens abandon politics, we give the special interests added means and opportunities. Motive, means, and opportunity, as we know from TV police dramas, are the three elements of a crime. When we abandon politics, we invite special interests to commit crimes. And we are the victims.

Anyone who seeks change or reform – any reform, on any issue, whether relatively minor or truly fundamental – has to find ways to attract, engage, inspire, and motivate ordinary Americans. Large numbers of ordinary Americans, enough to put real pressure on our elected officials. That's most challenging for political reforms, because so many of us are particularly turned off to the nuts and bolts of the political process — issues such as campaign finance, ballot access, and voting systems. And yet the political process is the key to progress on health care, education, global warming, and every other issue or problem.

Advocates of reform, any reform, will be much more likely to succeed if they start their campaigns by calling for Citizen Policies.

Democracy

Democracy is taught in school, part of the core curriculum in American history and social studies. Many of us study it also in college classes in government, politics, history, law, philosophy. Every American knows the basics, or should know them:

- Fair elections; one person, one vote.

- Majority rule, with strong protections for the rights of minorities.

- Checks and balances, safeguarding the integrity of the legislative, executive, and judicial branches.

- Due process, an independent judiciary, and respect for the rule of law.

- Government of the people, by the people, and for the people.

That's the theory.

In reality, however, a lot of us don't vote. In non-presidential elections, turnout is sometimes less than 10 percent. Many citizens are not even registered to vote. State and local elections are sometimes uncontested. Campaigns are absurdly expensive and funded by special interests. Political ads distort issues, misrepresent candidates, and mislead voters. Lobbyists write legislation. Congress sometimes votes late at night, without any opportunity for public review of the bill. Ordinary citizens have far less access to their elected representatives than do CEOs, celebrities, lobbyists, and campaign contributors.

One way to understand our situation is to view the core ideas as if they are subjects in school — democracy school. The semester is over. It's time for a report card. What grades would you give?

In Fair Elections, low voter turnout might justify a C. Recent elections have been marred by serious problems with voting machines, so a D might be appropriate.

In Majority Rule, members of the majority might assign a B+. Many members of minorities have a different experience, and are likely to give our democracy a D, or even an F.

Checks and Balances are currently quite weak. The president generally gets his way with both Congress and the judicial branch. Perhaps that gets a C- or D.

For Due Process, it's necessary to consider controversies about the rights of free speech, privacy, and habeas corpus, along with inconsistent and unjust use of the death penalty. That grade might be a D.

Our democracy apparently needs remedial education. More accurately, of course, it's not our democracy that's failing. It's us. We ordinary Americans, most of us, need remedial education in citizenship.

"One person, one vote" has to mean more than voting. All citizens ought to have relatively equal opportunities to participate in the ongoing process of democracy, not just at the ballot box. That means equal access to elected officials. Also equal opportunities to propose legislation, and equal opportunities for our proposals to be considered and debated. You, after all, as a citizen, are supposed to be equal to any celebrity or billionaire. Don't you agree? Doesn't that seem right, fair, sensible, democratic?

Elected officials meet with Bill Gates, Oprah Winfrey, Bono, Tim Russert, Angelina Jolie, Rush Limbaugh, and other celebrities. Lobbyists for big corporations get their phone calls returned. In contrast, when we ordinary citizens contact our representatives, the typical response is a form letter.

Perhaps it's time to admit that our government is really not a democracy. It might be more honest and accurate to call it an oligarchy, a government by the few, or a plutocracy, a government by the wealthy. Or a dollar-ocracy. Or a corporate-ocracy. Or a special-interest-ocracy.

Or – because elected officials have so much power to define issues and set agendas; and because they write election laws, regulate themselves, and even set their own pay and benefits, and because they have such opportunities to raise campaign money and increase their name recognition, and because many of them stay in office for decades – perhaps it's most accurate to describe our government as an elected dictatorship.

Are you content with our government? Do you feel well and truly represented?

If we sincerely want a democracy, a healthy democracy, a first step is to make sure every American can afford to participate. "One person, one vote" will be much more meaningful after we enact Citizen Policies. We individual citizens, working together, will finally be able to create a government of the people, by the people, and for the people.

Free People and Free Markets

When you hear politicians talk about "the market" or "the free market," what do you picture or understand? What do those terms mean to you?

We're told frequently that free people and free markets go together. In and through the market, we individuals are free to make choices, to pursue happiness. Buyers and sellers act according to their self-interest. Prices are determined by supply and demand. The process is self-regulating, as if by an "invisible hand." These ideas come from Adam Smith and *The Wealth of Nations*, the founding text in modern economics. For proponents of free markets, Smith's book is the bible.

Markets are supposed to be wise, powerful, trustworthy. *Trust the market*, business leaders tell us. *Let the market decide. Rely on the market, and it will provide health care and education. It will solve urban sprawl, global warming, and other problems.*

Markets are presumed to be most free, and people are therefore most free, when government is not involved. Conversely, people and markets are less free when government is large or more active, when government regulates markets. Freedom requires smaller government and less regulation. Trust the market, but not government. The market will let us be free. Government regulates and restrains us.

Is that what you've heard? Is it what you believe? Does it make sense to you?

The Wealth of Nations was published in 1776. The market Smith described, praised, and promoted was small-scale and local. Buyers and sellers were farmers and other self-employed individuals. Goods and money were exchanged directly. Transactions affected only the participants and their families. Participants lived near one another, and had ongoing contacts and relationships.

In modern markets, buyers and sellers are often on different continents. Most buyers and sellers are corporations, not individuals. Goods typically go through several intermediate transactions, from one corporation to another. Money typically goes through intermediate transactions involving banks and credit cards. The items that are bought and sold include stocks, bonds, currency, mortgages, credit card debts, and other financial instruments, and those transactions are often speculative. Traders also speculate on oil, land, gold, corn, cotton, and other commodities. A single transaction can affect millions of people around the world.

The market Smith wrote about was a farmers' market or flea market. Your local farmers' market is very different from the New York Stock Exchange. It's also very different from Wal-Mart. Most of the stuff at Wal-Mart is made in China and other low-wage countries; the actual seller is not the local store, but the corporate headquarters in Arkansas.

Champions of the market usually ignore these differences. They claim that all markets operate in the same way. They also ignore the fact that markets are undemocratic, inherently so, even antidemocratic. Markets are discriminatory. The very rich have more access and influence than ordinary individuals. People without money don't count at all. Corporations, which are legally defined as "fictitious persons," have more access and influence, more power, than *real* persons. Very big corporations – Wal-Mart, Microsoft, ExxonMobil, Citibank, and such – have enormous power; they shape, define, and can manipulate markets.

Markets will be more free and more fair after we enact Citizen Policies. Individuals and small businesses will all be able to participate and compete. We the People will be able to eliminate subsidies to big corporations. Subsidies distort markets, so eliminating subsidies will let markets function more efficiently and reliably, more freely and fairly.

The market, ultimately, is us, individual people. We are the market. Corporations, whether big or small, global or local, are only intermediaries. We individuals, by enacting Citizen Policies, can reclaim our economic and political power.

No More "Jobs"

Jobs, jobs, and more jobs, politicians promise. *Elect me and I will create jobs. Reelect me, because I created thousands of jobs, and I will create more.*

Government efforts to create jobs started with Franklin Roosevelt during the Great Depression. As part of his New Deal, government became the "employer of last resort." Government built roads, dams, schools, bridges, airports, national monuments, all with the goal of putting Americans back to work. Government hired writers, painters, photographers, and other artists, giving them jobs that used their talents.

Creating jobs directly is now out of favor. Pundits and politicians denounce such programs as "liberal" and "big government," using those terms as code words for socialism. That leaves two indirect methods: tax cuts for the rich and subsidies for big business. Tax cuts are supposed to stimulate investment and thereby to accelerate job creation. Subsidies have many names and forms, including tax credits, loan guarantees, enterprise zones, tax increment financing, and eminent domain. Both methods are endorsed by Democrats and Republicans, conservatives and liberals.

Have you ever started or run a small business? Have you managed a division, office, or franchise for a mid-size or large company? Think about that experience. Or think about people you know who own or manage businesses, and imagine yourself in their place. Have you hired many workers? When you hire someone, what is the situation? What's involved or required? What are your concerns?

One thing every business owner or manager knows: Hiring is expensive. It costs money to advertise, interview candidates, and train someone. It takes time. It's risky. The new person might not work out. Months or years can pass before the new person is adding enough value to offset the costs and risks.

Smart businesspeople *avoid* hiring. Business owners typically work 50, 60, 70, or more hours a week, even when they can afford to hire someone. Instead of hiring, owners and managers prefer to get current employees to work harder, faster, or longer. Right? Many of us know this from experience as owners or managers. Just about all of us know it, also, from being employees, from competing for a job, from being asked or forced to work overtime. A business that hires excess people would soon be out of business.

For the purpose of creating jobs, subsidies and tax cuts are inefficient, inherently inefficient. Employers know it's better and more profitable to *not* create jobs. Investors know it, too. Stock prices go up when companies lay off workers. CEOs get bonuses after firing workers. With subsidies and tax cuts, moreover, there are no guarantees that the money will go toward new jobs. Many companies use the money to raise CEO pay, buy back company stock, invest in other companies, or build lavish new headquarters. Wealthy individuals who get tax cuts can use the money to speculate on stocks, currency, or commodities; such speculative "investments" do not create jobs. Politicians who call for subsidies and tax cuts to create jobs, therefore, are actually asking businesses to be less businesslike, less focused on the bottom line.

Citizen Policies will put government out of the business of trying to create jobs; there will no longer be any reason to expect it to do that for us. Every citizen, including the unemployed, will have income for food and shelter. We'll be able to demand – and get – government that is lean, efficient, cost-effective. Our government, like a private business, will only create those jobs that are really necessary for it to function. Government officials will be able to focus more effectively on our real goals, needs, and values.

Businesses will benefit as well. Businesses will no longer be burdened or distracted by political pressures to create jobs. Small businesses will benefit most of all, because there will no longer be government subsidies to Wal-Mart, General Motors, and other big companies.

For creating jobs, moreover, Citizen Dividends will be much more effective than current approaches. A lot of us will start our own businesses. Starting a business will be much less risky when personal economic security is guaranteed. Our friends and family members might invest. Start-ups and small businesses create jobs far more rapidly and successfully than big companies. Politicians who sincerely believe in creating jobs might use that as a reason to call for Citizen Dividends.

It's important to consider the question of jobs, also, from an individual perspective, to make these matters personal. We depend on our jobs for our survival. We need jobs in order to earn money for food, shelter, health care, and so on. Our dependency allows politicians to use the promise of jobs to attract our votes. Our dependency allows big corporations to use the promise of jobs to coerce elected officials into giving them subsidies. Employers can coerce and exploit workers, threatening layoffs, demanding overtime.

Citizen Dividends will ensure that everyone has some income independent of any job. We will no longer be bound by our need for jobs; those chains will be broken. We ordinary citizens will be more free. We ordinary citizens will have more dignity.

Hot-Button Issues

Do you want to ban abortion? Or protect it as a right?

Permit same-sex marriage? Or amend the Constitution to make it illegal?

Ensure that law-abiding citizens can have guns, and perhaps carry them in public? Or regulate guns to reduce the risk of street crime, suicides, family violence, and random shootings?

Abortion, same-sex marriage, and gun control – and immigration, stem cell research, prayer in schools, aid to Israel, flag-burning, and the death penalty – are called "hot-button" issues because many of us respond predictably, automatically, like when someone pushes a button or flips a switch. Pushing the buttons, most politicians know, can motivate people to contribute, volunteer, and vote. These are also called "wedge" issues, because politicians use them as wedges to divide us. Driving the wedges and pushing the buttons, politicians know which voters to target with ads in support of an issue. They also know to avoid or downplay these issues with other voters.

On each side of every hot-button issue, of course, are interest groups. These issues are great for fundraising. Some single-issue special interest groups – such as the NRA, NARAL, and AIPAC – are very well-funded and powerful. They have lots of lawyers, lobbyists, PR professionals, and administrative staff. They raise lots of money for political campaigns.

Many of us are passionate about one or more of these issues. We care, deeply. That's why it's easy for the interest groups to manipulate us. The groups are very skillful, very practiced at using inflammatory statements, literature, and videos. They play their issues like bugles to get us to charge on command.

Have you ever given money to any issue group? Have you signed their petitions? If so, the Democratic and Republican parties probably know about it. Both parties maintain massive computer databases. They gather information on our magazine subscriptions, church attendance, shopping habits, contributions to charities and nonprofit organizations, and more. They know where you live, how much you earn, and what kind of car you drive. They have ways to use that information in order to craft personalized appeals; it's called "microtargeting" and it's practically a science.

Is banning or permitting abortion more important to you than your economic security? Are guns or gay rights, for or against, more important than your family's health care? More important than education? More important than global warming and climate change?

The interest groups hope so. Each group wants us to focus on its issue primarily. They push our buttons to keep us focused and to distract us from other issues or concerns. Focusing too exclusively and being distracted too easily, however, are characteristics of children. Grownups, especial-ly parents, have to know how to juggle competing concerns and demands. The interest groups treat us like children. They profit from our passions and our ignorance, our weakness and vulnerability.

Citizen Policies will remind us monthly that we are adults, citizens, responsible participants in our society. Abortion, gay rights, immigration, and other hot-button issues will still stir people's passions. These issues will still be featured in political campaigns. We, however, will be able to assess issues thoughtfully — and that's the key to real progress.

Politicians as Performers, Politics as Theater

People who run for office are typically well-known in advance. Some are very rich businesspeople. Some are famous actors or athletes. Some are spouses or children of elected officials. When the Democratic and Republican parties recruit candidates, they zealously seek people with high name recognition — or enough money to buy name recognition.

In addition, politicians gain a competitive edge if they know how to:

- Look and sound good on television.

- Look and sound sincere, authentic, optimistic, self-confident, trustworthy, likeable.

- State clichés, slogans, and platitudes as if they are original and profound.

- Respond to questions, any questions, by repeating scripted "talking points."

- Stay "on message" while talking at length; and conversely, talk at length without saying anything "off message."

- Appear to listen, even if only pretending to listen.

Political campaigns apply sophisticated marketing, advertising, and branding strategies. Issues and policies – and candidates, too – are packaged as products. The products are tested and polished, using focus groups and other techniques. Political campaigning is marketing. Politics, in many ways, is marketing.

Vote for Adams, he'll keep you safe.

Baker has an attractive family, and they go to church every week.

Vote for Charles, because she's a woman (or black or Latina).

You'd be comfortable having a drink with Davis, or having Davis as a neighbor.

Political marketers use many of the same methods that work to sell cars, cosmetics, and pharmaceuticals. Buy this, and you'll feel better. You'll feel safer. You'll be more secure. Buy this, it will make you more attractive. It will make happy. When marketing products, policies, and politicians, the focus is on appearances. Good packaging and superficial appeal – visceral, emotional appeal – is what sells. Emotional appeals are generally more effective than logic and evidence. Emphasizing emotions and appearances, also, is a way for political marketers to avoid discussing issues and policies.

Another way to avoid issues is by using negative ads: *We can't trust Adams because in the past he said or did something bad.*

Baker has accepted lots of money from special interests.

Charles will appoint the wrong people.

Davis flip-flops on the issues.

Negative ads work. They grab our attention and leave lasting impressions. Some negative ads are like horror movies, portraying the opponent as a monster. Be afraid. Be very afraid. *If my opponent is elected, we'll be attacked. You'll lose your job. Terrorists. Rapists. Job-killers.* Then, after scaring voters, candidates portray themselves as action heroes. *Only I can keep you safe. And I will.*

Political rallies and other campaign events are designed for TV cameras. The stage is set with close attention to the backdrop, lighting, and other theatrical details. Ordinary people who attend such events are like extras on a movie set. The extras hold signs, repeat chants and slogans, cheer and applaud on cue. The extras are part of the set. They're props. A small number get speaking roles, get to ask questions, though the questioners are usually vetted by the campaign and their questions are often scripted.

It's entertaining. It can be exciting. But is it democracy? Is this a sensible way to make important decisions about our lives, our world, our government? No. We the People are not the audience or part of the scenery. We're the producers. Citizen Policies will make it easier for us to fire performers who fail to follow our directions.

Advocates of Citizen Policies won't need slick packaging and professional marketing. Advocates will be able to campaign successfully as regular people with real ideas.

The Privileges of Elected Officials

Elected officials make a lot of decisions with minimal advice or guidance from the public. Minimal attention, too. Unless an official does something criminal, scandalous, or extremely stupid, public attention is normally positive. Elected officials are deferred to, catered to, indulged.

Whenever something good happens, elected officials take credit. When something goes wrong, they blame political rivals or predecessors. Or they blame circumstances beyond their control, circumstances that could not have been anticipated. Most politicians appear to be unwilling or unable to admit they are ever wrong. Say something often enough, they seem to believe, and it must be true or will somehow become true. Say something often enough, and other people will believe it and vote for the politician who says it.

In elections, incumbents have enormous advantages. Elected officials have extraordinary access to the media — far more access than their opponents and far, far more access than ordinary citizens. That access allows officials to define the issues, set the agenda, control the discourse, increase their name recognition. Media access and name recognition make it much easier for them to raise money. Incumbents raise campaign money throughout their terms, not just at election time. While campaigning full-time for reelection or higher office, moreover, incumbents are being paid with our taxpayer dollars.

In many towns, cities, and states, there is no political competition, no two-party system. One party rules. Incumbents are reelected after only token opposition. Some stay in office for decades, and then a spouse or child takes their place.

One-party rule and entrenched incumbents are very good for the special interests. Lobbyists get to know the officials, their staff members, consultants, and families. Those relationships are worth a lot to the lobbyists. Most of us like doing business with people we know, after all, and many of us do favors for our friends. Some lobbyists have prior relationships or family connections with the officials they lobby. Many lobbyists are former officials, lobbying their former colleagues.

These privileges are operative even in local government. Have you ever attended a meeting of your town or city council? What about your county government? Are meetings broadcast on community television? Do you watch? Ever?

At most meetings there are a few citizen activists. There are a few journalists. And there are a bunch of lawyers and lobbyists who represent real estate developers, major landowners, financial institutions, and large retail corporations. Official public meetings are usually just formalities. They're formal settings for presenting decisions that were made in private. Meetings are routine. Scripted. Boring. It makes sense that few of us bother to attend.

Occasionally, of course, citizens are inspired by some issue. When citizens turn out in large numbers, they often win. In towns and cities across America, citizens have saved parks and farmlands; blocked plans to increase taxes; stopped the construction of roads and shopping malls; and secured funding for schools, police, and other public services.

Citizen victories, however, are often short-lived. Special interests have many ways to get what they want. After any setback, they launch new PR campaigns, threaten lawsuits, threaten to take their jobs to another town or state, meet with friendly officials to renegotiate the deal. They sometimes get state or federal officials to intervene on their behalf, even to change state or federal law. When real estate developers want to build a new highway or airport, for example, they use these tactics and often spend many years and millions of dollars on lobbying.

The privileges of elected officials are proportionately greater at the state and national levels. The president and prominent members of Congress are celebrities; so are some governors and state legislators. They have automatic access to the media. They set the agenda for the nation. Their goals, desires, aspirations, and whims affect all of us. They are, moreover, extremely skillful at selling themselves and their policies; that's how they got elected to high offices.

Elected officials write the laws that regulate elections. State officials draw the boundaries of election districts, choosing the voters who are most likely to choose them and other members of their party. Redistricting and election regulations are powerful tools to maintain one-party rule. In most cases, though, the tool is bipartisan. It's a racket to protect incumbents.

Redistricting nearly determines who gets elected president. Because of the electoral college and one-party dominance in most states and the District of Columbia, a majority of Americans have no real say. Democratic and Republican candidates focus their campaigns almost entirely on Florida,

Ohio, and a few other swing states. The rest of us are basically bystanders.

The elected official with the most power and privileges, of course, is the president. The president manipulates the media in many ways. Journalists, pundits, editors, and publishers crave access; their jobs and careers depend on it. The president can deny, withhold, or limit that access, or threaten to do so. The president can select and reward journalists by granting exclusive interviews, or simply by calling on them at press conferences. So journalists have concrete incentives to provide favorable coverage. They have other incentives, too, particularly the vanity and prestige that come with access.

For the president and other prominent officials, privileges extend like a beach umbrella. Advisors, consultants, friends, and family members are covered. They have access to the officials. They have influence. They gain prestige and privileges by association. Journalists seek them out.

People who have privileges tend to believe they are special, free to act with impunity, above or outside the law. In fact, "privilege" literally means "private law." Privilege is antidemocratic.

Our democracy will be strengthened by the equality inherent in Citizen Policies. We ordinary citizens will be more equal with our elected officials. We'll be able to rewrite the rules of government and revoke some of our public servants' privileges.

Special and Not-so-special Interests

It's easy to identify elite special interests. Just listen to politicians when they criticize their opponents. Republicans attack Democrats for being beholden to labor unions, trial lawyers, gays and lesbians, Hollywood, and Silicon Valley. Democrats describe Republicans as being in the pockets of oil companies, the insurance industry, the NRA, Christian fundamentalists, and Wall Street.

Other powerful interests – real estate developers, big media corporations, the pro-Israel lobby, and military contractors – give money to Democrats and Republicans. Some very rich individuals also contribute to both. They're hedging their bets, guaranteeing their access. By giving money to both major parties, moreover, they avoid being criticized by either.

Special interests favor incumbents. Even highly partisan interests contribute money to incumbents of the other party. That's obvious when a political party loses the majority; a lot of special interest money reverses direction and flows the other way. Money follows power. And power seeks money. The reversal was dramatic when the Democrats won control of Congress in 2006.

In 2007, Hillary Clinton and Barack Obama each raised more than $100 million, while other presidential campaigns raised tens of millions; that was just 2007, before the first caucus or primary. Candidates for Congress raise millions or tens of millions, and so do gubernatorial candidates in large states. Other state office campaigns raise hundreds of thousands, or a million or more, and that includes judges in some states. In addition, the Republican and Democratic parties raise tens of millions of dollars each year, even non-election years. The Republican and Democratic parties also get millions of our taxpayer dollars for their presidential campaigns and conventions. A lot of money is raised by "bundlers" who solicit contributions from their friends, family members, colleagues, and other individuals, and who then get credit from the campaign.

Follow the money. Some of it goes to campaign managers, media consultants, lawyers, and other political professionals who work for or with the Democratic and Republican parties. Even more goes to owners of TV stations, radio stations, major newspapers, and cable companies. The media corporations, not surprisingly, downplay or dismiss any suggestion that they're biased by political money. The money talks, however, and tells a coherent story. Big media corporations, incumbent politicians, and the Democratic and Republican parties are uniquely privileged, powerful special interests. They work hard – and work together – to maintain the status quo.

The campaign finance system is thoroughly corrupt, yet perfectly legal. Politicians craft their platforms to appeal to wealthy special interests. The special interests give money to the candidates who say the right things. Elected officials have strong incentives to deliver on those promises in order to raise money for their reelection. Perfectly legal, because it's all out in the open. There's no need for secret deals or promises, no bribery or express quid pro quo.

Special interests are most powerful when they're organized in distinct groups or associations, and well-funded by members and donations. The groups have leaders – whether hired, elected, appointed, or self-appointed – and those leaders enjoy various privileges. Their privileges include access to elected officials and the media. Acting in the name of the group and its members, leaders decide which candidates the group will fund or endorse.

Special interests, however, are really not so special. Most of us work for big corporations. Many of us are Democrats or Republicans. We're churchgoers, union members, business owners, gun owners, seniors, members of professional associations. Many of us are in several of these categories. Thus, almost everyone is a minor player in one or more special interests.

The power of the special interests comes from us. When special interest groups and their leaders act on our behalf, it's only because we let them, we defer to them, we fail to make decisions for ourselves, we fail to stand up and assert ourselves when our interests are contrary to the group.

Each of us is greater than any specific interest. Each of us is greater than the sum of our interests. With the economic security of Citizen Policies, it will be easier for us individuals to perceive and pursue what's best for ourselves and our families. We won't be so dependent on interest group leaders, elected officials, and other prominent personalities; we won't be so predisposed to follow them. We'll be able to reform the campaign finance system to serve the common good, our mutual interests.

Conservative? Liberal? Both? Neither?

Do you call yourself a conservative? A liberal?

Is there some other political description that you prefer for yourself: moderate, independent, pragmatic, progressive, populist, radical, traditional, libertarian? None of the above? Do you use a more elaborate term, such as "fiscally conservative and socially liberal"?

Liberals believe in government. They cherish Social Security, Medicare, and other programs and policies of Franklin Roosevelt, John F. Kennedy, and Lyndon Johnson. They think new or expanded government programs are necessary for progress on homelessness, health care, education, global warming, and other issues or problems.

Conservatives believe in the market. They dislike government and distrust it, though they believe it has a duty to help preserve traditional values. They want to cut taxes and reduce the size of government, except for national security and the military, which they support absolutely and want to strengthen. They revere Ronald Reagan above all, and perhaps Barry Goldwater and Milton Friedman.

Isn't that what you hear from politicians and pundits? Is that how you understand and use these terms?

Liberal vs. conservative, or left vs. right, correlates only roughly with Democrats vs. Republicans. Most Democrats are moderates, and some describe themselves as conservatives. Many Republicans also claim to be moderates. In Republican party primaries, candidates often call their opponents "liberal."

The labels are awfully simplistic. They distort and trivialize political discourse. They also obscure the fact that political definitions change over time. There are fads and fashions in politics, just as there are in art, music, and other aspects of our culture. Some past Republican presidents were undeniably liberal by today's standards: Theodore Roosevelt, Dwight Eisenhower, Richard Nixon, and Gerald Ford.

"Conservative" means traditional, cautious, disposed to maintain existing institutions or conditions. Does that describe you? Almost all of us are conservative in some ways and situations.

"Liberal" means tolerant, generous, open-minded, seeking equal rights and liberties for all people. Aren't those values we aspire to live by? Values we teach our children?

Most of us are both conservative and liberal, in some ways one, in some ways the other. So are Citizen Policies. Individuals will be free to decide when and how to be traditional, cautious, deferential to the past, conservative; when and how to be tolerant, generous, seeking a better future, liberal. With our economic security guaranteed, we won't be so distracted by the labels, so manipulated by the self-serving pronouncements of politicians and pundits.

Using current conventional definitions – conservative vs. liberal, government vs. the market – Citizen Policies are neither. The common labels ignore individuals. Neither government nor the market can do anything, neither even exists, apart from us ordinary individuals. Citizen Policies will give us individuals more political and economic power.

In our political system today, special interests dominate both major parties and both ideologies. It's conservative special interests vs. liberal special interests, special-interest Democrats vs. special-interest Republicans.

Citizen Policies will transform politics. The playing field will be more level, guaranteed. Special interests will no longer have so many unfair advantages. Political debates, processes, and practices will no longer be bound by the old labels and definitions. The new politics: We the People vs. the status quo, ordinary individuals vs. the status quo.

Part Four
Now

A little rebellion, now and then, is a good thing, and as necessary in the political world as storms in the physical.

Thomas Jefferson

It does not take a majority to prevail. But rather an irate, tireless minority, keen on setting brushfires of freedom in the minds of men.

Samuel Adams

The people can never willfully betray their own interests; but they can be betrayed by the representatives of the people.

James Madison

There are more instances of the abridgement of the freedom of the people by gradual and silent encroachments of those in power than by violent and sudden usurpations.

James Madison

We must disenthrall ourselves, and then we shall save our country.

Abraham Lincoln

A great democracy must be progressive or it will soon cease to be a great democracy.

Theodore Roosevelt

There can be no perfect democracy curtailed by color, race, or poverty. But with all we can accomplish all, even peace.

W.E.B. Du Bois

Politics ought to be the part-time profession of every citizen who would protect the rights and privileges of free people and who would preserve what is good and fruitful in our national heritage.

Dwight Eisenhower

When once a republic is corrupted there is no possibility of remedying any of the growing evils but by removing the corruption...every other correction is either useless or a new evil.

Thomas Jefferson

23

I the Citizen

What do I want for my neighborhood, my community?
What do I want for my town or city? For my state? For our
nation?

These are questions each of us ought to ask often. Ask
and answer. And discuss with family members, friends, and
neighbors, perhaps modifying our answers as we learn from
other people's ideas and concerns.

This process is vital for democracy. We the People starts
with I the citizen. There is no *we* without more than one *I*,
and no We the People without a majority of citizens. There
is no *we*, except superficially, unless each *I* agrees to be
included. There is no We the People – it's just rhetoric – unless
a majority of citizens work together as citizens.

I the citizen, each of us thinking about our neighborhoods, our towns or cities, our states, our nation, thinking
and talking about what we want, listening to and learning
from our friends and neighbors, working together, compromising when necessary, and selecting, instructing, and
managing our representatives: that's democracy. That's how
it works. Democracy starts with individual citizens.

Pursuing Happiness

"What do I want?" is a question about self-interest, obviously. A core assumption in politics and economics – and marketing and advertising – is that people are motivated by self-interest. Self-interest is also central to our national identity — it's the pursuit of happiness, an unalienable right.

"What do I want for our nation?" is quite different from "What do I want for myself and my family?" These are different types of questions because we have different types of wants. For myself and my family, I may want a new car, a nicer home, a comfortable retirement, a tropical vacation, to send my children to elite universities. These are personal desires, and can generally be pursued without any significant impact on other people, most notably without harming other people. Such personal desires, in addition, can often be satisfied with money. When we have enough money, we can buy what we want. Money is what economists, politicians, and marketers use to measure self-interest, because money is quantifiable.

But no one can buy what he or she wants for our nation. Not even Bill Gates. What anyone wants for our nation can only be pursued with and through other people. To get what we want for our nation, we have to work together. That means politics.

Money is a very crude measure of happiness. It cannot provide or account for the real richness of our lives — our relationships with family and friends, our preferences regarding how and where to live, our faith traditions and moral values. Such wants, desires, and needs cannot be measured and quantified. Self-interest *cannot* be reduced to money.

Each of us has an immediate self-interest in fresh air and clean water; our health depends on it. Each of us has a self-interest in knowing that everyone we come in contact with has access to adequate health care; we don't want avian flu, staph infections, drug-resistant tuberculosis, or other infectious diseases we don't even know about. Each of us has a self-interest in good schools, and not just for our own children; it's important for everyone that all children are educated, because children grow up to be voters whose decisions affect all of us. Each of us has a self-interest in good roads, safe air travel, attractive parks and recreation areas, an effective police force and trustworthy justice system. Each of us has a self-interest in slowing climate change and achieving world peace.

Self-interest, in other words, is not just selfish. Pursuing happiness is not just personal. Real happiness involves other people. Real happiness requires healthy communities and a healthy environment. Appreciating this truth – that self-interest is more than money and possessions – can help us be happier.

My Government

Each of us has a self-interest in an accountable, democratic government. Whether we like government, hate it, or try to ignore it and hope it will just go away, we depend on it. Even people who view government as a "necessary evil" are admitting that it is necessary. Yet most of us talk about *the* government, which suggests some remote and self-contained entity, instead of *my* government or *our* government.

Government is necessary, most fundamentally, to protect property. That's why we have armed forces, police, laws, and courts. Without government, it would be impossible to accumulate property. We would not have money, at least not reliable money, nor could we rely on the banking system. We would not have roads, airports, the postal system. Markets could not function. Big corporations could produce toxic products and waste with impunity. There would be no patents and trademarks to protect intellectual property and promote invention and innovation. Government is a major source of our wealth and health and happiness.

If I do not participate actively in politics, I am merely a client or customer of government, a consumer of the services it provides. Sometimes I may be its victim, suffering the consequences of its abuses, excesses, or failures. As a citizen, however, I am much more than a client, customer, or consumer. I am a stakeholder or shareholder. I have rights and responsibilities.

Voting is not enough. If I don't vote or if the only thing I do is vote, I am agreeing to an elected dictatorship. I'm telling elected officials they can do whatever they want until the next election. That's obviously risky, indeed foolish and self-destructive, because politicians are so good at pursuing their own interests and not so good at serving ours.

Each of us has to decide: Participate as a citizen. Or live with the consequences of not participating.

What's best for my neighborhood, my community? What's best for my town or city? My state? Our nation? If I do not participate in making the decisions, someone else will make them for me — probably someone who doesn't even know me, someone who isn't thinking about my needs and interests. At this moment, in fact, many people are making decisions that affect me. Those people are not just government officials, they're executives with big corporations. A lot of us are affected, perhaps many millions of us, whenever a CEO decides to close a factory, whenever a real estate developer decides to build a strip mall, whenever a Wall Street tycoon decides to invest overseas instead of domestically.

All politics is personal, and that's as it should be. It's good for us individuals and good for our communities to make politics personal. That's particularly true when we understand self-interest in all its dimensions. Making politics personal helps us focus on democracy and be serious about it.

Who knows what's best for me and my family? My family and I do, of course. But my family and I depend on our government, local, state, and federal. My ability to do what I choose depends on what my government does. Our government is our only protection against being abused and exploited by big corporations. Our vigilant participation in politics is our only protection against being abused and exploited by our government.

It's *my* government, each of us ought to insist. What do I want from it? What do I deserve? What am I prepared to do in order to get the government I want and deserve?

24

Peaceful, Positive Revolution

Change. Reform. Progress. Hope.

These are words politicians use all the time. With most politicians, however, the words are just slogans. For every politician who promises change, there's another who's promising a competing change. For every change that sounds good and necessary to one person, there's another person who feels threatened. And there are special interests that resist any change. No politician, no matter how sincere and talented, can bring real change — unless We the People and we individuals are working together to achieve the same goals.

Real change will come with Citizen Policies, real reform, rapid progress, reasons to hope. We can solve our social, cultural, environmental, economic, and political problems.

Enacting Citizen Policies will be more than a political revolution. It will be a revolution of values. The status quo, because it's familiar, appears superficially to be right, so most of us tend to ignore or reject evidence that it is a mess of policy failures. As we consider Citizen Policies, each of us will have to question many of our assumptions. Each of us will have to acknowledge our roles in maintaining the status quo. That will be challenging, soul-searching. This revolution, however, despite the challenges, can be peaceful, positive, even joyful. It will be an opportunity, indeed a series of opportunities, for us to advance our values and affirm our humanity.

Do these ideas make sense to you? Do you think we should seriously consider them? Do you think we should at least discuss enacting Citizen Policies?

Can you see how an extra $500 to $1,000 a month, every month, for each adult citizen will help poor families meet critical needs and help middle class families realize their dreams? Can you see how this will help unite us — and help us get the government we want?

More personally: Can you see how this will help you and your family? What could this mean for the quality of your life today? How might it affect your dreams, hopes, and plans for the future? Are you willing to work actively to make it happen?

This revolution has to start with ordinary citizens. No charismatic leaders are required, nor does it make sense to wait for one. A revolution that starts with ordinary individuals will be much more democratic and much, much more likely to succeed.

You can make a big difference — a unique contribution.

Attracting Individual Allies

The first thing each advocate of Citizen Policies should do is find one or two allies. It's a lot easier to succeed with any goal when two or three people, or more, are working together as a team.

Finding allies may take a bit of time, patience, and gentle persistence. A common reaction to new ideas, after all, is to reject them. Knee-jerk objections are likely: *It sounds like socialism. We can't afford it. Why should we give any money to Bill Gates? Why should we give any money to people who are lazy, alcoholic, or addicted to drugs?* And so on.

For winning people over, time can be more effective than reasons or arguments. The most effective response to objections and doubts, in many cases, is simply to wait. Resume the conversation another day. It's good, second, to encourage people to question their own objections, to doubt their own doubts. Objections and doubts mostly echo conventional biases, not thoughtful analyses, and yield to respectful questioning. Too many of us default or defer to the status quo out of habit; knee-jerk objections are often just convenient rationalizations. A third good response is to point out to people that their objections are strengthening the status quo by reasserting it. But the status quo is indefensible. Current policies are not working.

Citizen Policies provide a real practical alternative to the status quo, and presenting an alternative is a necessary step toward any reform. If people have doubts or concerns, we can ask them to suggest different versions or modifications. Smaller Citizen Dividends? Larger ones? Eliminate government programs quickly, or cut only modestly while protecting current beneficiaries? Make Citizen Service mandatory? What do you think? What makes sense to you? These are the conversations we should be having.

A good way to attract allies is to tell the story of earlier efforts to guarantee economic security. Very few Americans know that history, and people like a good story. Similar ideas were extremely popular in the 1890s, 1930s, and 1960s, and each era brought us closer to enacting some plan. Telling the story is a way to suggest that now is the time, to say we must not miss this opportunity.

You might cite Thomas Jefferson, Thomas Paine, Henry George, Franklin Roosevelt, Milton Friedman, or Martin Luther King Jr. By mentioning them and other great Americans who supported some kind of guaranteed income, you will in effect be inviting people to join that group and help make history.

Reaching Out to Organizations

In most organizations, two or three members can present an idea and get it on the agenda for a discussion or possible endorsement. Good places to do this are churches, synagogues, and other faith communities. Christian, Jewish, Muslim, and other traditions maintain that we have a moral and religious duty to provide for the poor, a duty to seek justice and pursue it. Faith communities can be very influential.

Every city has clubs or networks of self-employed people and small business owners. Such people and organizations are likely allies because they know they're being hurt by current policies that subsidize big corporations. They're likely allies, in addition, because such people are entrepreneurial, looking for new ideas and opportunities. Many of them will have useful skills to help us spread the word.

In every city, also, there are activist groups working for civil rights, social justice, health care reform, education reform, environmental progress, and peace. Such groups will benefit from aligning their goals with Citizen Policies. After years or decades of signing petitions, attending meetings, sending letters to the editor, and so on, group members know that customary tactics are hard work, time-consuming, and rarely successful.

Other existing networks of grassroots power are labor unions, and there are good reasons for unions to join the campaign. Unions had real political clout for much of the 20th century, but declined significantly during and after the Reagan years. Calling for Citizen Policies will be a way for unions to renew their influence and restore their prestige. More important, Citizen Dividends will provide every worker with a personal strike fund. Workers will have more power as individuals and collectively.

Each organization that endorses Citizen Policies will make it easier for other groups to join the campaign.

Working with Political Parties

Are you an active member of a political party? If so, you might work within it and through it, crafting a version of Citizen Policies that upholds your party's core values. Even though the Democratic and Republican parties, separately and together, represent the status quo, both parties have mavericks and visionaries who may be very excited about these ideas.

Democratic versions can emphasize civil rights and egalitarianism. Advocates might cite Franklin Roosevelt, with his "Four Freedoms" and "Second Bill of Rights," along with Lyndon Johnson and the President's Commission on Income Maintenance Programs, George McGovern, and Jimmy Carter. Republican versions might focus on tax reform and states' rights. They might look to Abraham Lincoln and his support for the Homestead Act, Theodore Roosevelt and his reform agenda, Richard Nixon and the Family Assistance Plan, and Ronald Reagan's declarations about reducing the size of the federal government and trusting ordinary people.

The Green Party, Libertarian Party, and other "third" parties might use Citizen Policies in their efforts to become the second party, or the first. The Green Party of the United States already calls for a guaranteed basic income, as do Green parties around the world, and Green versions might emphasize the prospects for rapid progress on environmental and social justice issues. Libertarians might recognize the power of Citizen Dividends to achieve broad support for significant cuts in government. A Libertarian version could list dozens of local, state, and federal programs they want to eliminate, while describing the increases in personal liberty. There are many other "third" parties, and each might craft its own version with its own rationale.

Politicians, regardless of their political party or the office they seek, will be able to combine other goals, programs, and aspirations with Citizen Policies, thereby inspiring and motivating people to work together to achieve those goals. Local politicians may be leading advocates, because Citizen Policies will facilitate rapid progress on education, traffic congestion, sustainability, property tax reform, and other local issues that conventional approaches cannot solve.

Local politicians who are planning to run for higher office may be especially enthusiastic. Ordinary citizens, our elected representatives, and the political parties will be more able and likely to work together for the common good — while working to enact Citizen Policies and afterward, when we have them.

Mobilizing Supporters

Traditional forms of grassroots pressure – petitions, letters to the editor, letters to elected officials, meetings with officials – are effective when they endorse a specific policy, instead of just opposing something. A primary goal is to gain support from elected officials, whether by winning over current officials or defeating them and electing our allies. Campaigns can happen in every town and city around the country at the same time.

The weeks just after an election can be particularly good times to campaign because that's when officials are setting their agendas and priorities. Extra efforts will also be useful before Congress votes on any major tax or spending bill. If we already had Citizen Policies, would that spending be necessary? Could that tax be more fair and simple? We can use questions such as these, contrasting current actions and policies with the Citizen Policies alternative, to keep ourselves and other advocates focused and mobilized.

There may be situations where more direct actions are appropriate. Are politicians promising to create jobs and meeting with CEOs of big corporations? Advocates might assemble large groups to visit politicians' offices and attend public meetings. Are your taxpayer dollars being used to subsidize a hotel, highway, airport, or stadium? Protests and sit-ins at construction sites can attract the news media and educate large numbers of people. In such situations, however, it's important to avoid personal attacks and remember that people are just doing their jobs. Our goal as advocates is to educate everyone, secretaries and CEOs, construction workers and company owners — everyone.

Winning the Campaign

The key to a peaceful, positive revolution is to do it through the ballot box. Elect just a few people to Congress, one Senator and one member of the House of Representatives, and they can introduce a bill. In any state, elect a few legislators and perhaps a governor, and they can propose to test Citizen Policies at the state level. In any city or county facing the possible closure of a military base, elected officials can push the federal government to go ahead with the closure and distribute part of the savings to local residents.

Getting a bill introduced is a key step — and that's when advocates have to multiply our efforts to attract allies, reach out to organizations, work with political parties, and mobilize supporters. Special interests are very good at delaying the legislative process. They can get their friends to send the bill to a committee that rarely meets, and then to subcommittees, and then to schedule hearings that are postponed indefinitely. Special interests can also introduce competing bills with complex provisions designed to minimize reform. Special interests profit from every delay, and we have to stay engaged in order to thwart their efforts.

Another key is compromise. That's an important lesson from the defeat of Nixon's Family Assistance Plan, which moderate Democrats and moderate Republicans voted for in the House. Liberal senators refused to compromise. They were being prodded by a powerful activist group, the National Welfare Rights Organization, which was demanding more generous benefits. If the liberal senators and NWRO had been willing to compromise, America would have had a guaranteed income in 1972.

There will be huge rewards for the people who lead the campaign, especially for the politicians who run for office on this platform. The president who signs the law will almost certainly be more revered than Ronald Reagan and Franklin D. Roosevelt. He or she might even be acclaimed as one of our greatest presidents, with George Washington, Thomas Jefferson, and Abraham Lincoln.

25

Our Lives, Our World, Our Government

What government do I want? What government do you want? What government do We the People want? These are questions the Founders asked, and their answers are in the Declaration of Independence and the Constitution.

Asking and answering these questions, today, is necessary to repair our broken government. Our lives and our world depend on our answers. *Our* answers, not the politicians' answers, nor the pundits' or journalists' or CEOs' answers; letting other people answer for us is how our government got broken. The Founders fought for the right of the people to alter or abolish their government — and according to the Declaration, we have a duty to alter or abolish a government when it is destructive of our safety and happiness.

Citizen Policies will change everything. We get to start anew, to make our government over again. While we're enacting Citizen Policies and from then on, we individuals and We the People will have meaningful opportunities to ask fundamental questions about our government, to discuss our answers, and to decide what we want to do. In addition – and unlike today – we'll have real power to act on what we decide.

Getting Started

We'll have to compromise on the amount of Citizen Dividends. Some of us will want it to be less than $500 a month, to avoid undermining people's incentives to work, earn, and produce. Others will prefer $1,000 a month or more, to ensure that single parents have enough money. We might be guided by the federal poverty level, which the U.S. Census Bureau sets at $20,650 for a family of four. Citizen Dividends of $861 a month would provide $20,664 a year for a couple, just enough to end poverty. Compromise. See how it works. Then we can adjust the amount if necessary. There can be local supplements in places where the cost of living is especially high.

Suppose we start with $500 a month. That's $6,000 a year. There are roughly 190 million citizens age 18 or over, according to the U.S. Census Bureau, so the total cost would be $1.14 trillion a year. Sounds like a lot of money, but it's affordable in a federal budget of $3 trillion — easily affordable if we get serious about tax reform and cutting programs that become superfluous.*

It makes sense to combine this with tax reform. Citizen Dividends can replace the current standard deduction and exemptions. We'll be able to eliminate the Alternative Minimum Tax, replace the EITC, close lots of loopholes, and

---

* Appendix 2 has more information about how we can pay for Citizen Dividends.

eliminate lots of provisions that are designed to promote specific behavior, such as saving for retirement, going to school, and buying energy-efficient cars and homes. The purpose of taxes, after all, is to raise money to fund our government, not to be the carrots and sticks of public policy. Simplify the tax code, and taxes will just be taxes.

With tax-free Citizen Dividends in place of the standard deduction, it would make sense to have a flat income tax that is truly flat, applying to all income from any source. Or we could have something between a true flat tax and the current system. There might be, say, a 20 percent tax on all income up to $60,000, a 25 percent rate on income from $60,001 to $200,000, and a 35 percent rate on all income above that. The principle of flattening and simplifying the tax code, in addition, can help us decide what to do about the estate tax, corporate taxes, and other taxes and tax policies.*

With any such tax reform, distributing Citizen Dividends will be easy, efficient, and cost-effective. We could eliminate withholding for income up to $20,000 or more, depending on the amount of Citizen Dividends. More of our earnings will go directly into our pockets. Low-income workers and nonworkers will get payments directly from the government, a negative income tax, which could be deposited directly into bank accounts. Simple. Easy to administer. Much simpler and easier to administer than the current system.

Soon we might implement other reforms, such as increasing taxes on consumption of natural resources. We might shift to consumption taxes primarily, perhaps phasing out the income tax. That or any other reform will be much more feasible than today.

*Appendix 2 illustrates a flat income tax combined with Citizen Dividends.

Cutting Government

Most efforts to cut government uphold the status quo. Proposed cuts normally seek only to change government priorities and reduce spending by some percentage, not to return to the Founders ideal of limited government. Throughout the budget process, special interests defend the status quo and reinforce it. That's why it's almost impossible for proponents of smaller government to get very far. Politicians promise to shrink the government, and a lot of us vote for them because of those promises — but regardless of whom we elect, the government gets larger.

Citizen Policies will help us put the status quo on the defensive, reversing the burden of proof. Is this program, agency, or department still necessary? Why? Defenders of the status quo will have to make their case. They'll have to show that the program, agency, or department serves some necessary purpose. If they can't show the need, and we might ask them periodically to document it, we can cut the budget to zero. We can eliminate programs and agencies, even whole departments.

A good place to start cutting government will be to eliminate all spending that seeks to create jobs. Our government will no longer be in the business of creating extra jobs for anyone. Our government will no longer be in the business of providing corporate welfare and subsidizing private employers. Corporate welfare is hard to calculate; there's no set definition and it's primarily state and local. Common estimates are around $250 billion per year.

When each of us has guaranteed income for food and shelter, we'll be able to cut or eliminate, for example:

- welfare programs in the Department of Health and Human Services;

- subsidies for foreign trade provided by the Department of Commerce;

- spending in the Department of Energy, Department of the Interior, and other departments and agencies that promote exploring, drilling, and mining for minerals and fossil fuels;

- job-training programs – which are actually indirect subsidies to future employers – in the Department of Labor and Department of Education;

- public housing programs in the Department of Housing and Urban Development — government-owned housing units can be sold, perhaps to current residents; and

- the overall waste and job-creating excesses in the Department of Defense.

That's just at the federal level. Parallel agencies exist in every state and can also be cut. Whether programs are eliminated quickly and completely or only gradually will depend on social and political conditions and on the size of Citizen Dividends. Larger dividends will facilitate faster, deeper cuts.

When people talk about cutting government, they commonly focus on Social Security and Medicare. The big entitlement programs are growing, eating up the federal budget at an accelerating rate. Status quo practices are unsustainable and everyone knows it, but politicians are afraid to call for any specific reform because they know that specific proposals antagonize special interests. Reform will become much more feasible after we have Citizen Policies.

Strengthening Our Democracy

Election reform has been a hot topic in recent years, primarily because the flaws and problems have been so evident. Citizen Policies will make it much easier for us to implement meaningful reforms. Should we have full public funding of elections? Full, prompt disclosure of all campaign contributors, including those that support supposedly independent groups? A requirement that contributions come from individual citizens only, not from corporations, labor unions, or political action committees? Require media outlets, as a condition of their licenses, to give free airtime to all qualified candidates?

Should we abolish the electoral college? It's clearly undemocratic, but abolishing it would require a constitutional amendment, and many states benefit from the status quo so that's nearly impossible. We can achieve the same goal much more quickly and easily through the National Popular Vote, an interstate compact among states that agree to give all their electoral votes to whoever wins the popular vote nationwide. It's fully constitutional, and will only go into effect after it has been approved by enough states to control a majority of the electoral votes. It would prevent, forever, the awkward and demoralizing situation our country endured in the still-disputed election of 2000, when the loser of the popular vote got the most electoral votes.

Should we reform the presidential primary system? It's a mess, and it thwarts our democratic interest in thoughtful deliberation and examination of the candidates. One idea is to have very small states hold their primaries or caucuses in March, mid-size states in April, larger states in May, and the largest states in June. But that or any reform – and many have been proposed and should be considered – will be hard to accomplish because elections are controlled by the states and the two major parties, with the states competing to maximize their influence. If we want a more rational system, We the People have to work within the political parties and with our national and state governments.

Should we reform our winner-take-all elections? One alternative is working, strengthening democracy and promoting more active citizen participation in San Francisco and other cities, and has been debated in several state legislatures. It's called Ranked Choice Voting or Instant Runoff Voting. Voters go to the polls and mark ballots with their first choice, second choice, third choice, and so on. If no candidate gets more than 50 percent of the votes on the first round, the candidate with the fewest votes is eliminated, and voters for that candidate have their second choices counted. The process continues until someone receives more than 50 percent and is declared the winner. Nobody ever holds office with less than majority support. And every candidate has incentives to reach out to all voters and seek to be at least the second or third choice of every citizen.

Should we have automatic voter registration when someone turns 18? Automatically restore voting rights to people released from prison after they've paid their debt to society? Same-day voter registration, as in Maine, Minnesota,

Montana, New Hampshire, and a few other states? Make election day a holiday? Have elections on weekends? Vote by mail? Make voting mandatory, as some other countries do?

A good start toward reform would be to make election administration truly nonpartisan. "Nonpartisan" has to mean exactly that, as distinct from "bipartisan." Currently, presidential and congressional elections are managed by the Federal Election Commission. The FEC consists of three Democrats and three Republicans, and its rules require a majority vote, so in many cases it cannot even act; that's what "bipartisan" usually means, a racket that serves the interests of elected officials and the two major parties. Roughly 40 percent of us are not members of either major party. We the People should restructure the FEC and similar agencies in the states to ensure that independent voters and third parties are represented proportionally and have equal opportunities to get onto ballots and into debates. We should also create nonpartisan commissions to delineate election districts, taking that responsibility away from partisan officials who are primarily concerned with keeping themselves and their party in power.

Something else we have to do is extend full citizenship rights to the 600,000 residents of the District of Columbia. Currently, the District is actually a colony, ruled by the U.S. Congress in much the same way that the original 13 colonies were ruled by the British Parliament. Congress imposes policies on District residents, overriding actions by the elected D.C. government. This violation of democracy has been condemned by many countries, international agencies, and the United Nations.

On these questions and others, we ordinary citizens will be able to have good, meaningful, productive discussions — and we'll be more able to enact reforms that make sense to a majority of us. We'll be able to demand that our elected representatives serve our interests, not the special interests. Our democracy will no longer be so dominated by the special interests of elected officials and the Democratic and Republican parties.

Regulating Corporations

When the Founders declared America to be free and independent, they were seeking to overthrow not only King George III and British rule, but also corporations chartered by the British government. Remember the Boston Tea Party? The tea the rebels threw into the harbor was owned by a global corporation, the British East India Company. Shareholders included the King and members of the House of Lords, and they got subsidies from the British government in the form of troops that protected their property and profits. There were subsidized British corporations throughout the 13 colonies. Some colonies were chartered as British corporations.

Today – at this moment, in fact – CEOs of big corporations are making decisions that affect you and your family, your neighborhood, your town and city, and those CEOs might be anywhere in the world. However, thanks to the Founders, We the People are sovereign. We have the right to assert our sovereignty over corporations that abuse or exploit us. We just need the will and the wisdom to direct our government to regulate corporations effectively.

Corporations often claim to be socially responsible, environmentally responsible, "corporate citizens." That's good marketing, apparently. But it is naïve, indeed absurd, for us to expect corporations to value our long-term needs and interests. They can't. Corporations exist to produce value for shareholders. If a corporation fails to maximize quarterly profits, stock prices fall, shareholders can sue, the CEO can be fired. Social, cultural, environmental, and political values are secondary at best, and often contrary to the corporation's core mission.

We the People have to regulate corporations through our national government, our state governments, and perhaps also our local governments. We have to demand that our elected representatives pass the necessary laws and enforce them.

Do you think your local government should be able to regulate foreign corporations? Should foreign corporations be banned from participating in local political campaigns? Would you like local government agencies to give some preference to local small businesses when purchasing supplies? If any of that makes sense to you, too bad. Big corporations with big budgets for marketing, lobbying, campaign contributions, and lawsuits make such local policies impossible, just as the World Trade Organization undermines our federal government's ability to set international trade standards for the United States.

Regulations can actually be good for markets and corporations, especially if the regulations are relatively simple, without loopholes. Reliable regulations, with real penalties for any violation, can make market conditions more predictable. Predictable market conditions make it easier for businesses to plan and compete, and more likely that the most innovative and efficient businesses win.

One way to think about regulating corporations – how to regulate effectively, and why we must do so – is to picture We the People as parents and corporations as young children. Wise parents make rules and set limits. They know that rules and limits help their children grow and learn from their mistakes. Parents have to make sure their children don't break things, eat too many cookies, or harm themselves or other people. We the People have to stop corporations when they abuse or exploit individuals, our communities, and our environment. Sometimes we have to discipline and penalize the corporations, even revoke their charters. Currently, however, we depend on corporations to provide jobs, food, housing, transportation, and so on, and our dependency gives the corporations significant economic and political power over us. It's like letting the kids control the household budget.

We'll have more autonomy and control when each of us has some income independent of our jobs. We'll be acting like wise parents when we eliminate subsidies to corporations. Eliminating subsidies, moreover, will by itself reduce the need for regulations. The playing field will be more level for small, local businesses.

Another way we can reduce the need for regulations is to increase consumption taxes on natural resources. It will cost more for corporations to buy fossil fuel, timber, steel, land, and other materials, so they'll use resources more efficiently, with less waste and less pollution. If they're not producing waste and pollution, we won't have to regulate it.

Governing the Courts

In order to assert our sovereignty effectively over corporations, We the People have to assert our sovereignty over the courts. Judges and courts sometimes impose their own ideas, interpretations, and policy solutions; politicians call it "judge-made law," and denounce the "activist judges" responsible. But it seems that people get angry only when they disagree with some specific action. Social conservatives *want* judges to ban abortion, same-sex marriage, and affirmative action. Liberals *want* judges to guarantee these practices as rights, and to rule against any limitations or restrictions. Rulings on these and other issues are denounced by one side as activism, and praised by the other side as restrained and constitutional.

An example of judge-made law – a unique example, because both conservatives and liberals ignore it or endorse it – is "corporate personhood." Corporations claim to have the rights that are affirmed in the Constitution, including the rights to free speech, due process, and privacy. Courts routinely recognize those claims, even though the Constitution does not mention corporations and our federal government has not passed any laws giving these rights to corporations.

Through most of America's first century, state legislatures granted few corporate charters. Corporations could be formed only for a specific purpose that provided some public benefit, such as a road, canal, bank, or university, and corporations were not allowed to buy other corporations or to own land except for the specified purpose. Charters were granted for a limited period only, and states revoked charters when corporations exceeded their authority. As America industrialized in the mid-1800s, a few people became quite wealthy. Wealthy bankers and industrialists published newspapers, funded political campaigns, filed lawsuits challenging state and local regulations, and lobbied legislatures to relax the laws regarding corporations.

During the Civil War, some people and corporations became vastly wealthier and more powerful from supplying the Union army with weapons, uniforms, food, and other supplies. After the war, the Fourteenth Amendment was written to give equal rights to former slaves. It was ratified in 1868, and corporations promptly began filing lawsuits claiming that it applied to them also, because they were "persons." One case, *Santa Clara County v. Southern Pacific Railroad Co.*, involved the railroad's refusal to pay property taxes. The company lost in lower courts and appealed to the Supreme Court. In 1886, the court decided that the Fourteenth Amendment applied to corporations. That's judge-made law. In fact, it was not in the actual court decision, only the headnotes when the decision was published, yet it is cited as a legal precedent.

Corporations are not persons, they are not citizens, and using either word to describe them is a fraud. Corporations don't breathe, eat, or sleep, and they operate 24 hours a day, perpetually. We need fresh air, clean water, healthy food, loving relationships, and livable communities; corporations sometimes profit from providing these needs, and sometimes profit from violating or manipulating them. We are pursuing happiness, which is complex, changeable, and individualized; corporations only pursue profits for shareholders. We are created by God and nature; corporations are created when government bureaucrats approve their charters.

The main bulwark for corporate personhood is a legal doctrine: *stare decisis,* which is Latin for "to stand by things decided." *Stare decisis* is the legal basis and argument for defaulting to the status quo. The courts used *stare decisis* for many decades to perpetuate the racist notion that it was legal to have separate facilities for blacks and whites. The courts for many decades obstructed equal rights for women. As we saw with civil rights for blacks and women, however, mass social movements are the way to get courts to overturn precedents. The courts will respond when We the People mobilize and demand action.

We the People have to abolish corporate personhood, much as earlier Americans abolished slavery. It will not require a civil war, only lawsuits, legislation, and perhaps amendments to our state constitutions. Regardless of what it takes, we have to do it. The status quo is unjust and anti-democratic. The sooner we act, the better.

Our efforts to govern the courts are impaired by the fact that many states elect judges and many of those judges accept contributions from special interests. We individuals have to be attentive to judicial elections and selections, while being critical of the role special interests play in that process. That's an added burden, obviously, and an added reason to welcome the increased citizen participation we can expect with Citizen Policies.

Holding the News Media Accountable

The Founders guaranteed freedom of the press because they knew that journalists and government are natural adversaries. Government officials prefer secrecy, even if its only for convenience. Sometimes officials have something to hide, of course, and they have various ways to keep things hidden, including the use of complex, legalistic, bureaucratic jargon. The bureaucracies are massive and the volume of information is overwhelming. Journalists are our eyes and ears, and we depend on them to help us hold government accountable. The news media must remain independent, skeptical, and accountable to our needs as consumers of information.

We the People have to be vigilant, and have to support investigative journalists who serve the public interest — and Citizen Policies will help us invest the time and effort to do that. Overseeing our government is serious, necessary work. It's hard work, in particular, because government officials and agencies have spokespeople, consultants, and other media professionals operating full-time to make the politicians and agencies look good, honest, and competent. Our eyes and ears have to be open, actively looking and listening – and then asking questions, sometimes lots of questions – seeking the truth about what government officials are saying and doing.

We have to be vigilant in the other direction, too, overseeing the news media. Some journalists are practically stenographers for government spokespeople, just rewriting official press releases. Some journalists seem to believe their job is to interview both an elected official and someone from the other major party, a Democrat and a Republican, as if those two perspectives encompass the truth. That was clearly evident in the months before the U.S. invasion of Iraq. Leading Democrats supported the Bush administration, so the big media corporations ignored critics of the invasion or disparaged the critics. Instead of investigating and seeking the truth, many journalists, editors, publishers, and producers acted as cheerleaders.

There were no big media corporations in the Founders' time; their news media were only local and only newspapers. We live with radio, television, and the Internet – a 24/7 news cycle – and the media feed us a steady diet of celebrity gossip, sports scores, and fluff, crowding out real news that directly affects our lives. Owners and CEOs of big media corporations are rich, powerful, and privileged; have extraordinary access to politicians; and earn millions of dollars from political ads. Big media corporations decide which candidates to cover and which to ignore, and those decisions are often self-fulfilling. The candidates that are ignored cannot raise money, and the issues those candidates champion cannot get onto the public agenda. In these and other ways, big media corporations reinforce the status quo. We have to be vigilant, and it makes sense for us to get some of our news from alternative sources.

Most of us use the media primarily for entertainment, not for civic purposes, and media corporations are in business to make money. But we individuals and We the People have to insist that the news media, in exchange for the use of public airwaves and infrastructure, serve the public interest. We have to demand and ensure that the news media are vigilant, vigorous, and impartial in giving us the information we need to participate effectively in our democracy.

Rebuilding America

Hope, optimism, a can-do spirit: These have always been defining characteristics of America and Americans. They are the spirit of Citizen Policies, too, and Citizen Policies will revitalize that spirit throughout our nation.

Rebuilding America is necessary in the most literal sense. Our nation's roads, dams, bridges, and levees are crumbling and collapsing. We saw dramatic evidence of that with the levees in New Orleans and the I-35 bridge in Minneapolis. Shortly after that bridge disaster, the Federal Highway Administration announced that more than 75,000 U.S. bridges are "structurally deficient."

Our prosperity as individuals and as a nation in the 1950s and '60s was due in significant part to public investment in infrastructure, most notably the construction of the interstate highway system. Our prosperity and security in coming decades depend on similar investments today. Rebuilding bridges, levees, and other infrastructure, and building new high-speed railroads, is also a smart way to create jobs and stimulate economic growth. Public investment is vital, and political disputes about the details must be secondary. Acknowledging the need for investment will help us resolve questions about project selection, budgets, priorities, and so on, including whether the work should be done by government agencies directly or outsourced to private contractors with government oversight.

Rebuilding America must also include our civic infrastructure. We individuals have to regain our sense of being citizens. Civics and citizenship have to become, again, part of the core curriculum in our schools. Citizen Service can play a key role in that process. Within a year or two of enacting Citizen Policies, service will be a normal part of our everyday lives. It will be something we discuss with friends and neighbors, and will surely be a topic for gossip. Actors, athletes, and other celebrities will mention their service when they're interviewed in *Parade* and *People,* and when they appear on Leno and Letterman. So will CEOs and billionaires featured in *Business Week* and the *New York Times.*

An important step in rebuilding our nation and sense of community has to include caring for the troops who have served in Iraq, Afghanistan, and elsewhere. Government has to do its part, of course, perhaps with a new version of the G.I. Bill that paid for World War II veterans to attend college. Ordinary individuals must also be involved, particularly those among us who did not serve. Everyone can find appropriate ways to express our thanks.

Rebuilding America also means reaffirming our commitment to uphold the U.S. Constitution. Every president takes office with an oath from Article II, Section I: "I do solemnly swear (or affirm) that I will faithfully execute the office of President of the United States, and will to the best of my ability, preserve, protect and defend the Constitution of the United States." We individuals and We the People have to demand that our federal government renounce torture, restore Habeas Corpus, respect our Fourth Amendment rights to privacy, and renew our commitment to "liberty and justice for all."

Promoting Freedom, Democracy, and Peace

We the People might offer to help people in other countries enact their own versions of Citizen Policies. That can be the basis for a new foreign policy.

The idea of promoting freedom and democracy has been championed by Democrats and Republicans, from JFK to

Ronald Reagan, and this is sure to be the fastest and most effective way to succeed. Today, foreign aid is mostly used to promote trade and create jobs. That only helps a small handful of people. A lot of our aid goes to American corporations that are supposed to provide the jobs, and some of the money stays in the United States. Corporations based in Delaware, with CEOs who live in White Plains, get taxpayer money to pay for advertising in South Korea. That's probably not what Kennedy and Reagan had in mind when they talked about promoting freedom and democracy.

A primary goal of foreign aid – according to every recent Secretary of State, Democrats and Republicans – is to keep foreign governments stable and friendly toward us. We can accomplish that by promoting foreign versions of Citizen Dividends. When ordinary people in other countries have income for food and shelter, they'll have compelling reasons to want their own governments to be stable. Revolutions and military coups, after all, are most likely when people are hungry and insecure. A secondary goal, stated repeatedly by Secretaries of State Colin Powell and Condoleezza Rice, has been to procure cooperation in the "war on terror." Helping other countries enact their own Citizen Policies will surely accomplish that, as terrorist groups mainly recruit among the disenfranchised and promise material comfort to the families of suicide bombers.

With poor countries that are already democracies, our president and State Department can raise these ideas in meetings and public statements. We might offer to provide funds or administrative support. With authoritarian governments, we might stop aiding the central government – stop military aid, in particular – and announce that we're putting the money into some type of escrow account, to be distributed whenever the people of that country enact some basic income plan. We might insist that all aid to authoritarian countries be distributed by international agencies, such as the Red Cross. Whether we do these things quickly and publicly or more quietly and diplomatically will vary, of course, according to the unique situation in each country.

Stopping all military aid makes sense in any case. So does working with the United Nations and other international agencies to oppose all weapons sales and transfers. Citizen Policies in the United States is a necessary step because members of Congress often talk about creating jobs when they vote in favor of selling weapons. Roughly half of all weapons sold internationally are made in the U.S.A.

Another step we might take is to declare, unilaterally and unambiguously, that after any sort of military coup we will end all trade until after free elections have been held. Here, too, the major current obstacle to such declarations is the perceived need to promote trade and create domestic jobs. Citizen Policies will make us less dependent on those jobs. Those of us who are especially eager for progress might boycott global corporations that operate in repressive countries, and might urge our government to sanction the corporations.

Freedom, democracy, and peace are possible worldwide, perhaps fairly soon, if We the People make them a priority — a higher priority than government efforts to create jobs.

26

Now

"We mutually pledge to each other our lives, our fortunes, and our sacred honor." That's the conclusion of the Declaration of Independence. That's what the Founders signed. That's what each of them committed to. When they signed, moreover, each of them knew that they could be hanged for it.

What are *we* willing to pledge?

What are *you* willing to commit to?

At this moment, in the United States and countries around the world, people are suffering and dying from preventable diseases. People are being robbed and raped. There are wars and droughts and famines. Our air and water are becoming more polluted. Our planet is getting hotter and species are going extinct. Terrorists are meeting and plotting their next attack.

At this moment, too, tens of millions of people are working for some type of change, reform, progress. Advocates for change face huge obstacles, however, because most people are busy, or disenchanted with politics, or have simply lost hope. Most of us also seem to believe that change will come, somehow, if we just elect the right person. But every politician promises change, reform, and progress, and too often the only changes are the names and faces.

In order to achieve any meaningful reform, many millions of people have to work together. That's the major weakness in most reform plans: they don't offer anything that appeals directly and concretely to ordinary people's self-interest — yours and mine.

Would you like an extra $500 to $1,000 a month, tax-free? Would you like your spouse, parents, and adult children to also receive that?

Are you willing to expend a bit of effort to make it happen?

What kind of government do you want? Are you willing to act as a citizen, and to work together with other citizens and demand the government you want?

These are not just rhetorical or hypothetical questions. They're the type of questions the Founders asked and answered. They're questions the Founders thought every citizen in every generation should ask and answer.

Our situation is desperate and getting worse by the moment.

What are we waiting for?

Appendix 1:
Previous Attempts

Thomas Jefferson was the first American who sought to guarantee people's economic security. In 1776, while serving as a delegate to the Virginia legislature, he proposed giving 50 acres of public land to any propertyless individual willing to farm it. Many states subsequently enacted similar programs.

Thomas Paine published *Agrarian Justice* in 1795. The title page of the first edition summarized his proposal:

> Agrarian justice, opposed to agrarian law, and to agrarian monopoly. Being a plan for meliorating the conditions of man by creating in every nation, a national fund, to pay to every person, when arriving at the age of twenty-one years, the sum of fifteen pounds sterling, to enable him or her to begin the world! And also, ten pounds sterling per annum during life to every person now living of the age of fifty years, and to all others when they shall arrive at that age, to enable them to live in old age without wretchedness, and go decently out of the world.

Paine wanted the funds to come from a "ground-rent" paid by property owners. This is just and proper, he argued, because the earth is "the common property of the human race" and everyone deserves a share. Payments were to go to every person, rich or poor, healthy or disabled. It is "a right, and not a charity, that I am pleading for."

Abraham Lincoln called for, and the federal government enacted, the National Homestead Act of 1862. It granted 160 acres of public land to any head of a family 21 years of age or older who agreed to reside upon the land and cultivate it for five years. Almost 720,000 homesteads were established under the law, and homesteads continued to be available in some states until the early 1900s.

Henry George published *Progress and Poverty* in 1879, and the book sold more than two million copies over the following two decades. He sought to abolish all taxes on income or production, because such taxes discourage labor, and to replace them with a single tax on land. "There is a fundamental and irreconcilable difference between property in things which are the product of labor and property in land." In *The Land Question*, published in 1881, he called for "land-value" taxes to be high enough to confiscate unearned income and profits from speculation, and he claimed:

> There would be at once a large surplus over and above what are now considered the legitimate expenses of government. We could divide this, if we wanted to, among the whole community, share and share alike.

George was nearly elected mayor of New York City as an independent candidate in 1886. (The Republican who finished third was Theodore Roosevelt.)

Edward Bellamy, in an 1887 novel, *Looking Backward*, described how people might live in the year 2000 when society provides everyone with food, shelter, education, and health care. He envisioned an extraordinary increase in civility, generosity, and creativity. People around the United States formed more than 160 "Bellamy clubs" to discuss his ideas and to work toward implementing them. George's and Bellamy's books contributed significantly to the political ferment of the Populist and Progressive era, and to the many political reforms that were realized.

Francis Townsend, a family physician, wrote a letter to the editor of a Long Beach, CA newspaper in 1933, proposing government payments of $200 each month to everyone aged 60 or older. (That was the depth of the Depression, and $200 would now equal almost $2,800.) Townsend's "Old Age Revolving Pension" combined "liberal financial retirement for the aged with national recovery and permanent prosperity." The recovery and permanent prosperity were to be achieved by requiring recipients to quit any paid work and to spend all of the money each month, thereby creating jobs for younger workers.

Townsend published a pamphlet describing the idea, and in 1934 he testified in Congress. Over the next two years roughly 2.2 million people joined Townsend Clubs — and they played a key role in winning Social Security. A copy of Townsend's pamphlet is on the Social Security Administration's web site. www.socialsecurity.gov/history/towns5.html

Huey P. Long launched "Share Our Wealth" in 1934. He wanted to guarantee an annual income of $5,000 for every family, and proposed to raise the money through substantial taxes on the very rich. Share Our Wealth clubs were formed in every state, and in 1935 they claimed to have 7.7 million members. He was preparing to run for president against Franklin Roosevelt, but was assassinated by the son of a political rival.

Lewis Mumford's 1934 book, *Technics and Civilization*, examined the history of technology and its social impacts. He asserted that it is possible to provide everyone with the necessities for life, and that actually doing so is the only way to prevent social and economic instability.

Franklin Roosevelt, in his annual Message to Congress on January 11, 1944 and in a fireside chat to the American people the same evening, stated that "true individual freedom cannot exist without economic security and independence." To provide that, he proposed "a second Bill of Rights, under which a new basis of security and prosperity can be established for all — regardless of station, or race, or creed."

F. A. Hayek discussed economic security in his 1944 book, *The Road to Serfdom*. "There can be no doubt that some minimum of food, shelter, and clothing, sufficient to preserve health and the capacity to work, can be assured to everybody." This is "no privilege but a legitimate object of desire ... [that] can be provide for all outside of and supplementary to the market system." Doing so, he opined, would enhance everyone's freedom and security. He received the Nobel Memorial Prize in Economics in 1974.

Peter Drucker proposed a "predictable income plan" in *The New Society*, published in 1949 and reissued in 1960. Predictable income would "banish the uncertainty, the dread of the unknown and the deep feelings of insecurity under which the worker today lives." He rejected the idea of trying to guarantee jobs or wages. Any job or wage guarantee "would not be worth the paper on which it is written. It would give the worker the illusion of security which is bound to be cruelly disappointed" during economic downturns. Such practices could also "freeze the economy ... subsidizing obsolescent industries and restricting, if not stopping, technological progress." He wanted guaranteed incomes to be minimal and variable as economic conditions change.

The 1960s and '70s

Though the idea of guaranteed economic security sparked mass movements in the 1890s and 1930s, there was no such movement in the 1960s. Instead, social scientists were the main proponents. The mass movements of the late '60s focused on civil rights and social justice, including women's rights, and on ending the war in Vietnam.

Milton Friedman called for a "negative income tax" in 1962 in *Capitalism and Freedom* and in subsequent books and articles throughout his career. In *Free to Choose* (1980), he wrote:

> We should replace the ragbag of specific welfare programs with a single comprehensive program of income supplements in cash — a negative income tax. It would provide an assured minimum to all persons in need, regardless of the reasons for their need, while doing as little harm as possible to their character, their independence, or their incentives to better their own conditions.

Friedman was an economics advisor to Barry Goldwater in his 1964 campaign for president, served on Richard Nixon's committee of economic advisors, and got the Nobel Memorial Prize in Economics in 1976.

Robert Theobald, in a 1963 book, *Free Men and Free Markets*, proposed "Basic Economic Security" as an extension of Social Security to include everyone. He argued that it is necessary because computers and automation were replacing many jobs:

> The need is clear: the principle of an *economic floor* under each individual must be established. This principle would apply equally to every

member of society and carry with it no connotation of personal inadequacy or implication that an undeserved income was being received from an overgenerous government.

Theobald edited a 1966 book, *The Guaranteed Income: Next Step in Economic Evolution?* that included papers by **Erich Fromm**, **Marshall McLuhan**, and other eminent social scientists.

Philip Wogaman published *Guaranteed Annual Income: The Moral Issues* in 1968. As a minister and professor of Christian ethics, he asked, "Should we or should we not guarantee the basic material condition of human life as a social right of every man?" He concluded that we must do so for ethical reasons.

Lyndon Johnson appointed a President's Commission on Income Maintenance Programs in January 1968 to study the needs of poor Americans and make recommendations. Commission members included scholars, politicians, presidents of labor unions, and presidents of major corporations. It issued a unanimous report in November 1969:

> Our main recommendation is for the creation of a universal income supplement program financed and administered by the Federal Government, making cash payments to all members of the population with income needs. ... We do not believe that work disincentive effects of the proposed program would be serious.

The Commission opposed work requirements, stating that they "cannot be used effectively in determining eligibility for aid."

In the spring of 1968, five prominent economists – **John Kenneth Galbraith**, **Paul Samuelson** (1970 Nobel laureate), **Robert Lampman**, **Harold Watts**, and **James Tobin** (1981 Nobel laureate)

– called on Congress "to adopt this year a national system of income guarantees and supplements." They circulated a letter that was signed by 1,200 of their colleagues.

Also in 1968, the federal Office of Economic Opportunity began a series of experiments with guaranteed income in place of welfare. The experiments continued until 1975, with families in New Jersey, Denver, Seattle, and elsewhere – more than 8,500 people in all – receiving funds each month to keep them at or above the poverty level. Researchers tracked the number of hours people worked, the rate of divorce, and other variables. Divorce rates were the same as comparison groups. Overall work hours declined about 6 percent, though it was higher than that in some of the studies. Most of the decline was among wives and teenagers, not the men who were primary wage earners.

This was the largest social science experiment ever attempted, and the results continue to be disputed. There have been more than 350 scholarly articles by supporters and opponents of guaranteed income plans. Many reports are based on preliminary or partial results. Many popular reports and interpretations are biased, sometimes obviously so.

Martin Luther King Jr. called for guaranteed income throughout the final year of his life. His last book, published in 1968, was *Where Do We Go From Here: Chaos or Community?* In it he wrote:

> A host of positive psychological changes inevitably will result from widespread economic security. The dignity of the individual will flourish when the decisions concerning his life are in his hands, when he has the assurance that his income is stable and certain, and when he knows that he has the means to seek self-improvement. Personal conflicts between husband, wife and children will

diminish when the unjust measurement of human worth on a scale of dollars is eliminated.

King noted that more than two-thirds of the beneficiaries of guaranteed income would be white, and maintained that "the time has come for us to civilize ourselves by the total, direct and immediate abolition of poverty." That, he maintained, is necessary for lasting progress on housing, education, and civil rights.

R. Buckminster Fuller, in a 1969 book, *Operating Manual for Spaceship Earth*, described our present political and economic practices as leading toward self-destruction. To avoid that, "we must give each human who is or becomes unemployed a life fellowship in research and development or in just simple thinking." That would free everyone to "think truthfully and to act accordingly without fear of losing his franchise to live."

Daniel Patrick Moynihan was a domestic policy advisor to **Richard Nixon** and the primary author of Nixon's Family Assistance Plan. Moynihan's 1973 book, *The Politics of a Guaranteed Income*, described in detail how the plan was conceived, presented, debated, and ultimately defeated. He blamed the defeat on many factors, including Nixon's refusal to expend any political capital; the skillful maneuvering of conservative opponents in the Senate; the timidity and ambition of liberals in the Senate, who wanted an issue to run on in 1972; and the misguided, shortsighted actions of the National Welfare Rights Organization, which organized against the plan, seeking something more generous.

George McGovern campaigned for president in 1972 with an economic platform that called for a more generous and universal guaranteed income, "Demogrants." The plan was written by **James Tobin**.

Gerald Ford was the minority leader in the House during the debates on the Family Assistance Plan. He voted for it and defended it actively against conservatives' objections. After becoming president, he supported the EITC and signed it into law in 1975.

Jimmy Carter was the only southern governor to endorse Nixon's plan, and his call for comprehensive welfare reform was popular during the 1976 campaign. He tried to renew debate about guaranteed economic security with his Program for Better Jobs and Income in 1978, but he was unable to get much support in Congress.

The Alaska Permanent Fund Dividend

Oil was discovered in Alaska in 1969. **Jay Hammond**, a Republican, was the governor from 1974 to 1982, and he endorsed the idea of distributing some of the royalty income to residents. The state constitution was amended to create the Alaska Permanent Fund to benefit current residents and future generations. A percentage of all royalties goes into the Fund, which is permanent because the money is invested in a diverse portfolio, managed by a semi-independent corporation. Dividends are paid every year to every legal resident who was in the state for more than 6 months of the year.

The first dividend was paid in 1982, when every resident received a check for $1,000. The amount fluctuates every year, depending on the price of oil, the stock market, and general economic conditions. Dividends are paid in October of every year, as either a check or direct deposit into bank accounts. In 2007 the dividend was $1,654.

A similar fund exists in Alberta, Canada. Others have been proposed.

1980 to the Present

From 1978 until 2006, no prominent Democrat or Republican called for any effort to guarantee people's economic security. The country supposedly "moved to the right" and "became more conservative" — but that conventional wisdom may simply reflect the timidity of political elites and the narrowness of public discourse. If an idea is not discussed, after all, it cannot attract popular support.

A number of scholars, most of them independent, have attempted to restart the debate:

Leonard M. Greene published *Free Enterprise Without Poverty* in 1981 and *The National Tax Rebate: A New America with Less Government* in 1998.

Allan Sheahen published *Guaranteed Income: The Right to Economic Security* in 1983.

Philippe Van Parijs published *Arguing for Basic Income: Ethical Foundations for a Radical Reform* in 1992, *Real Freedom for All: What (if anything) can justify capitalism?* in 1997, and *What's Wrong with a Free Lunch* in 2001. (*Free Lunch* includes papers by a number of eminent social scientists, among them **Gar Alperovitz**, **Emma Rothschild**, and **Herbert Simon**, who received the Nobel Prize in Economics in 1978. There was a forward by **Robert Solow**, who received the Nobel Prize in 1987).

Robert R. Schutz published *The $30,000 Solution: A Guaranteed Annual Income for Every American* in 1996.

Michael L. Murray published *...And Economic Justice for All: Welfare Reform for the 21st Century* in 1997.

Steven Shafarman published *Healing Americans: A New Vision for Politics, Economics, and Pursuing Happiness* in 1998, *Healing*

Politics: Citizen Policies and the Pursuit of Happiness in 2000, and *We the People: Healing Our Democracy and Saving Our World* in 2001.

Bruce Ackerman and **Anne Alstott** published *The Stakeholder Society* in 1999.

Charles Murray published *In Our Hands: A Plan to Replace the Welfare State* in 2006.

In February 2001, there were huge surpluses in the federal budget. The **Congressional Progressive Caucus** called for an "American People's Dividend" of $300 for every citizen, including children, and they wanted the dividend to be repeated yearly if surpluses continued, as economists expected. The Progressive Caucus at that time was about 50 members of the House of Representatives and one Senator, Paul Wellstone. The plan attracted support from the AFL-CIO and other organizations, and Democrats in the House made it part of their tax proposal.

In the Senate, conservative Democrats insisted on only a one-time payment and only for adults who earned enough money to pay income taxes, and they included that version in their bill. The Bush administration and Republicans in both houses opposed the idea – their plan was to cut tax rates on capital gains and for people with higher incomes – but they accepted the Senate version, though only after the payments were made into advance rebates on 2002 income taxes. When the $300 checks went out in August, the Bush administration sent out letters claiming credit for the rebates — and most Americans, including journalists, accepted those claims.

In June 2004, the **Green Party of the United States** adopted a platform plank calling for a guaranteed basic income.

In 2005, several Democrats and Republicans in both houses of Congress introduced plans to use government funds to create "stakeholder accounts" for children at birth. Every child would get a savings account with government money, and poor families would be able to add money tax-free. At age 18, children would be able to use the money for education, to start a business, or to buy a home. The bill has continued to receive bipartisan support, though it has not yet passed any committee in either house.

In May of 2006, **Cong. Bob Filner**, a Democrat from San Diego, introduced H.R. 5257, the "Tax Cut for the Rest of Us Act of 2006." It would have provided a guaranteed basic income of $2,000 for everyone who files a tax return, plus $2,000 for the spouse of the person who files and $1,000 for each dependent child under age 18. That would have replaced the standard deduction and exemptions, and could have been implemented with only minimal changes in tax forms and policies. The bill attracted only a few co-sponsors, however, none of them Republicans, so it never advanced.

In the 2008 presidential campaign, indirect support for guaranteed economic security came from Republican **Mike Huckabee** and Democrat **Mike Gravel**. Both called for abolishing the IRS and implementing a national retail sales tax, the **Fair Tax**. The plan includes monthly cash payments based on household size. The proposed "prebates" are $196 for a single person, $391 for a couple, $525 for a couple with two children, and more than that for larger households. Though the amount is minimal – it's designed to offset the punishing effects of the sales tax on the poor – it would be a guaranteed income and could be increased.

Appendix 2:
Current Efforts

Citizen Policies Advocates is a nonpartisan, nonprofit organization that educates people about guaranteed economic security and facilitates the campaign to provide it for everyone. For more information please visit www.citizenpolicies.org

The **U.S. Basic Income Guarantee Network** is an informal network that promotes discussion of the basic income guarantee. USBIG welcomes people who are interested in any aspect of guaranteed income. Most members are academics – economists, sociologists, political scientists, and so on – and political activists are also welcome. **USBIG** was founded in 2001 and has held annual conferences each winter since 2002. The group also posts discussion papers on its web site, www.usbig.net

The **Basic Income Earth Network** was founded in 1986 as the Basic Income European Network. **BIEN** members changed the "E" in 2004 to recognize the fact that debates about basic income were occurring in the United States, Brazil, South Africa, Australia, Japan, and many other countries outside Europe. **BIEN** has a conference every other year. www.basicincome.org

Basic Income Studies is an academic journal. The first issue was published in June, 2006. It is published twice a year, and available online at www.bepress.com/bis

For information about other groups around the world – and there are many – visit www.usbig.net/links.html

How Are We Going to Pay for It?

Several people have presented basic income plans with analyses of how to pay for it. There are roughly 190 million citizens age 18 or over, according to the U.S. Census Bureau. The total cost of Citizen Dividends of $500 a month would be $1.14 trillion a year — that's definitely affordable. There's more than enough money available from cutting current government programs that become superfluous.

Debates about what to cut, how quickly, and how deeply, will be intense. Many compromises will be necessary. We'll be able to eliminate many programs completely, while cutting others in stages and evaluating the results. The important thing is to get started.

Irwin Garfinkel, Huang Chien-Chung, and **Wendy Nadich**, have done several analyses, most recently in February 2002. They simulate four basic income plans, with different benefit levels for adults, the elderly, children, and people who receive Social Security survivors and disability benefits. The alternatives "are designed to place a high percentage of families above the poverty threshold, whether the family has a productive (working) adult or not." They identified 115 existing programs that can be cut or eliminated. They concluded that any of their plans would "decrease poverty more effectively than the current system." Their analysis is discussion paper #14 at www.usbig.net/papers.html

Charles M. A. Clark started with the specific goal of ending (officially-defined) poverty in America — and designed his plan to do just that. So he selected a basic income for adults of $9,359, which is about $780 a month, plus $3,500 for children. The total cost would be nearly 2 trillion dollars a year. To pay for that and other necessary government functions, he proposed "a flat tax on all incomes, to replace the federal income tax, as well as the other remaining sources of federal government funding." The tax rate would be

35.2 percent, with no deductions or exemptions. The basic income would be tax-free. His 2002 paper is #80 atwww.usbig.net/papers. html

Charles Murray would provide $10,000 a year to every citizen age 21 or older. He seeks to end all other federal, state, and local programs that transfer funds, including Social Security, with a constitutional amendment to enforce the elimination of those programs. He would also eliminate Medicare and Medicaid; with the extra income people receive, everyone could afford medical insurance, and he would require everyone to buy it. His plan is in a 2006 book, *In Our Hands: A Plan to Replace the Welfare State,* which has detailed financial analyses in the appendix.

Allan Sheahen also favors a basic income of $10,000 a year, though for everyone age 18 or over. He found $1.52 trillion in potential savings, which is almost enough to cover the $1.9 trillion he estimated as the cost of his plan. Using official IRS numbers from 2004, he identified 138 tax loopholes, deductions, and adjustments that could be eliminated, with a total saving of $741 billion. Then he estimated the savings from eliminating the standard tax deduction and personal exemptions, an additional $244 billion. Third, he found more than 100 welfare programs that will not be needed, saving $375 billion. He then added $161 billion saved from cutting the defense budget from the current level back to its 2000 level. A complete list of the programs he would cut is in the appendix to his paper. (Without the defense cuts, his potential savings are $1.36 trillion.) His 2006 discussion paper is #144 at www.usbig. net/papers.html

Each of them examined only the federal budget, leaving out the savings from cutting state and local programs that also become superfluous. None of their proposals included the concept of Citizen Service and the benefits and savings it will provide. None of them attempted to measure the economic benefits of the social, cultural, and environmental progress we can expect. We can easily find the money to pay for Citizen Policies. We just have to find the political will.

Flat Income Tax Examples

A flat income tax has been the goal of many reformers for many years, but opponents have argued that it would hurt the poor, who have to spend a higher percentage of their income on basic necessities. Combining tax-free Citizen Dividends with a flat income tax would be fair, extremely simple, and good for just about everyone, rich and poor alike.

This combination gives us two variables, the tax rate and Citizen Dividends, and each can be adjusted to serve different purposes. Lower Citizen Dividends will allow low taxes. Higher Citizen Dividends will ensure that, for example, unemployed single mothers can afford food and shelter. Higher Citizen Dividends will also facilitate faster and deeper cuts in government programs. Each variable might be adjusted periodically, after elections, say, or automatically based on economic conditions.

To illustrate these possibilities, here are two tables. The first uses a 20 percent tax rate and Citizen Dividends of $6,000 a year, which is $500 a month. The second has a 40 percent tax rate and Citizen Dividends of $12,000 a year, which is $1,000 a month:

Total Income	Tax 20 percent	Citizen Dividends	Net Tax	Net Income	Net Tax Rate
0	0	6,000	-6,000	6,000	0
10,000	2,000	6,000	-4,000	14,000	0
20,000	4,000	6,000	-2,000	22,000	0
30,000	6,000	6,000	0	30,000	0
60,000	12,000	6,000	6,000	54,000	10 %
100,000	20,000	6,000	14,000	86,000	14 %
200,000	40,000	6,000	34,000	166,000	17 %
1,000,000	200,000	6,000	194,000	806,000	19.4%

Total Income	Tax 40 percent	Citizen Dividends	Net Tax	Net Income	Net Tax Rate
0	0	12,000	-12,000	12,000	0
10,000	4,000	12,000	-8,000	18,000	0
20,000	8,000	12,000	-4,000	24,000	0
30,000	12,000	12,000	0	30,000	0
60,000	24,000	12,000	12,000	36,000	20 percent
100,000	40,000	12,000	28,000	72,000	28 percent
200,000	80,000	12,000	68,000	144,000	34 percent
1,000,000	400,000	12,000	388,000	612,000	38.8 percent

The Debate about Iraq

On April 9, 2003, three weeks after the U.S. invasion of Iraq, the New York Times published an op-ed that proposed an Alaska-style fund for the Iraqi people. The author was Steven C. Clemons, Executive Vice-President of the New America Foundation in Washington, D.C.:

> Most revolutions that produce stable democracies expand the number of stakeholders in the nation's economy. ...
>
> Iraq's annual oil revenue comes to approximately $20 billion. A postwar government could invest

$12 billion a year in infrastructure to rebuild the nation. The other $8 billion could anchor an Iraq Permanent Fund, to be invested in a diverse set of international equities. The resulting income would go directly to Iraq's six million households. These payments would make a huge difference to families in a country whose per capita gross domestic product rests at about $2,500. ...

Establishing this fund would show a skeptical world that America will make sure Iraq's oil revenues directly benefit Iraqi citizens.

The op-ed is posted at www.steveclemons.com/A-AlaskaFundIraq. htm

On May 2, 2003, Secretary of State Colin Powell testified before Congress in favor of the idea, and said the Bush administration is considering it. On June 13, 2003, the polling firm John Zogby International released results of a poll showing that nearly 60 percent of Americans supported using oil revenues to compensate Iraqi citizens. On June 23, Paul Bremer, administrator of U.S. policy in Iraq, appeared before Congress and endorsed it. On July 11, Sen. Lisa Murkowski, a Republican from Alaska, and Sen. Mary Landrieu, a Democrat from Louisiana, introduced an amendment to another bill calling for a sense of the Senate resolution in support of creating an "Iraqi Freedom Fund."

Gov. Jay Hammond and other Alaskans actively promoted the idea in newspapers, videos, and web sites. There were news reports that members of the board of the Alaska Permanent Fund personally lobbied President Bush.

On September 10, 2003, the New York Times published a column by John Tierney:

> The same idea [is] in vogue among liberal foreign aid experts, conservative economists and a diverse group of political leaders in America and Iraq. The notion of diverting oil wealth directly to citizens, perhaps through annual payments like Alaska's, has become that political rarity: a wonky idea with mass appeal. ... The concept is also popular with some Kurdish politicians in the north and Shiite Muslim politicians in the south, who have complained for decades of being shortchanged by politicians in Baghdad.

Soon after that, however, the idea simply disappeared from public discourse. Perhaps some journalist will investigate what happened. Did Iraqi politicians debate it and reject it? Did someone in the Bush administration kill it?

Bibliography

Recommended Books, 1

This first list is books that focus primarily on guaranteed economic security. Different authors have different names for their plans, not surprisingly, including: basic economic security, basic income, basic income guarantee, basic income grant, Citizen Dividends, citizen's income, guaranteed income, guaranteed annual income, guaranteed livable income, national dividend, national tax rebate, negative income tax, predictable income, social credit, social dividends, stakeholder dividends, and "the Plan."

Ackerman, Bruce, and Anne Alstott, *The Stakeholder Society* (1999).

Funiciello, Theresa, *Tyranny of Kindness* (1993).

Greene, Leonard M., *Free Enterprise Without Poverty* (1998).

_____, *The National Tax Rebate* (1998).

Moynihan, Daniel Patrick, *The Politics of a Guaranteed Income* (1973).

Murray, Charles, *In Our Hands: The Plan to Abolish the Welfare State* (2006).

Murray, Michael L., *...And Economic Justice for All* (1997).

Paine, Thomas, *Agrarian Justice* (1793).

Schultz, Robert, *The $30,000 Solution* (1996).

Shafarman, Steven, *Healing Americans* (1998).

_____, *Healing Politics: Citizen Policies and the Pursuit of Happiness* (2000).

_____, *We the People: Healing Our Democracy and Saving Our World* (2001).

Sheahen, Allen, *Guaranteed Income: The Right to Economic Security* (1983).

Steensland, Brian, *The Failed Welfare Revolution: America's Struggle over Guaranteed Income Policy.* (2008).

Theobald, Robert, *Free Men and Free Markets* (1963).

_____, editor, *The Guaranteed Income* (1966). (Includes pieces by Erich Fromm, Marshall McLuhan, and others.)

Townsend, Francis, *Old Age Revolving Pensions* (1934).

van Parijs, Philippe, *Real Freedom For All: What, if anything, can justify capitalism?* (1995)

_____, *What's Wrong with a Free Lunch* (2000). (Includes responses by Gar Alperovitz, Herbert Simon, Emma Rothschild, Fred Block, and others, and a forward by Robert Solow.)

_____, ed. *Arguing for Basic Income: Ethical Foundation for a Radical Reform.* (1992)

Wogaman, Philip, *Guaranteed Annual Income: The Moral Issues* (1968).

Recommended Books, 2

These are books that mention – and recommend – the idea of guaranteed economic security, though they are mostly focused on other issues and reforms.

Alperovitz, Gar, *America Beyond Capitalism* (2005).

Barber, Benjamin R. *A Place for Us* (1998).

Daly, Herman, and John Cobb, *For the Common Good* (1994).

Drucker, Peter, *The New Society* (1950).

Friedman, Milton, *Capitalism and Freedom* (1962).

_____, and Rose Friedman, *Free to Choose* (1980).

Fuller, R. Buckminster, *Operating Manual for Spaceship Earth* (1969).

Hayek, F.A. *The Road to Serfdom* (1944).

Henderson, Hazel, *Building a Win-Win World* (1996).

Illich, Ivan, *The Right to Useful Unemployment* (1996).

King Jr., Martin Luther, *Where Do We Go From Here?* (1967).

Korten, David, *When Corporations Rule the World* (1995).

Rifkin, Jeremy, *The End of Work* (1995).

Robertson, James, *Transforming Economic Life: A Millennial Challenge* (1998).

Acknowledgments

This book is the product of 25 years thinking and writing, and many people encouraged me in some way. From the early period in Santa Barbara, I thank John Clausen, Elisa Gottheil-Luciani, Judy Shafarman, J. W. Ballard, Marne McGuire, David Knight Dow, Kathleen Gildred, Scott London, Harvey Bottelson, and Susie French. While writing my first book on these ideas, Robert Fitzgerald was an exemplary mentor, listening generously, reading drafts sympathetically, and questioning Socratically; thanks, Bob.

At the Fielding Institute doctoral program in Human and Organizational Development, thanks to Jeremy Shapiro, Richard Appelbaum, and Keith Melville. Thanks to Susan Shapiro and Kim Grant for helping me self-publish my first book on these ideas.

After I moved to Washington D.C., thanks to Ronnie Dugger, my fellow jailbird, for his editorial and political guidance. And to Doris "Granny D" Haddock, Chuck Collins, Pat and Lou Hammann, and the rest of the Democracy Brigades. Thanks also to George Ripley, Lorin Kleinman, and other members of the D.C. activist community. And to Gary Flo and Hanno Beck. Thanks to Iris Amdur for design and layout on *We the People*.

The U.S. Basic Income Guarantee Network has provided a virtual intellectual home, and a delightful community during our yearly conferences. Thanks to Karl Widerquist, Michael Lewis, Eri Noguchi, Almaz Zelleke, Fred Block, Jeff Smith, and just about everyone who's attended our meetings. Thanks also to Sen.

Eduardo Matarazzo Suplicy, Philippe Van Parijs, Guy Standing, and the members of the Basic Income Earth Network. Special thanks to Allan Sheahen for supporting these ideas and projects in many ways, and for supporting me personally.

Karin Hoffman at Tendril Press has been great, especially with the very tight production schedule. Thanks, Karin, for being so easy to work with and so committed to serving me and other authors. Thanks also to B.J. Dohrmann and many other people at CEOSpace.

Thanks most of all to Mike Livingston and Heidi Thompson: I could not have completed this book without you. Your editing and copyediting, Mike, has helped me become a better writer and more thoughtful citizen, and your friendship has been invaluable.

For you, Heidi, I cannot find the words to express my gratitude. You inspire me with your passion, playfulness, intelligence, and commitment. I'm blessed to have you in my life.

Index

Index to come with first full printing.

About the Author

Steven Shafarman is the founder and president of Citizen Policies Advocates, and a member of the coordinating committee of the U.S. Basic Income Guarantee Network. He is also the creator of *FlexAware*™ — a revolutionary system of exercise, fitness, and healing. This is his fifth book. He lives in Washington, D.C.

Share a copy of
PEACEFUL, POSITIVE REVOLUTION

Online orders: www.TendrilPress.com

Mail Postal Orders to:

Tendril Press

PO Box 441110
Aurora, CO 80044

Phone Orders: 303.696.9227

The price of each book is $16.95 plus applicable taxes.

USA shipping is $2.50 for the first book,
$1.50 for each additional book.

International shipping is $10.00 for the first book,
$5.00 for each additional book,

Check or Major Credit Cards accepted.
Card number: _____
Name on card: _____
Exp. Date: _____ CVC2 Code: _____
Signature: _____
Telephone: _____

Ship to:
Name: _____
Address: _____
City: _____ State: ____ Zip: _____
Email address_____
Telephone: _____

For more great reading visit www.TendrilPress.com